52 FAITH ADVENTURES
FOR DADS AND THEIR KIDS

ANDY FROST

To Dave
with love
Dad x

FATHERS DAY 2021

First published in 2021 by Care for the Family.

A catalogue record for this book is available from the British Library.
ISBN: 978-0-9955596-9-1

Designed by Lois Hillier Designs.
Page layout by AW Graphic Design.
Printed and bound in Great Britain by Xpedient Print Services.

Care for the Family is a Christian initiative to strengthen family life.
A registered charity (England and Wales: 1066905; Scotland: SC038497).
A company limited by guarantee no. 3482910. Registered in England and Wales.

CONTENTS

FOREWORD

USING THIS BOOK

TIPS FOR INTREPID ADVENTURERS

ADVENTURES

Why not use the boxes to tick off each adventure that you complete?

GREAT OUTDOORS

SEASONAL ADVENTURES

ADVENTURES AT HOME

EVERYDAY ADVENTURES

FURTHER RESOURCES

BIBLE OVERVIEW

FOREWORD

I wonder who or what helped shape the faith you have today? As I look back in my own life, I think of a Brazilian family who would often invite me round to their flat to eat pasta and play games. There was something infectious about their laughter and the joy they had in God. A World War Two veteran called Ron, who had escaped from a concentration camp, shared the most incredible stories with me whilst trying to teach me how to paint with acrylics. He taught me about God's faithfulness over the years. There were church youth workers who recognised my potential and gifting, and who helped me understand what it was to take risks for my faith. And then there was my mum, who showed me what it meant to put Jesus first, as each morning I would find her in bed reading her worn Bible, sharing the truths she had found.

Many people have played an important part in the development of my Christian faith. One of the most significant was my dad. We've all had different experiences with our dads. Mine, though not perfect, was a really positive experience. He died when I was in my twenties and I still miss him. In him I saw something of what it meant to follow Jesus.

Now, my dad was no Indiana Jones. He never trekked into deepest Africa dressed in khaki, searching out treasure. But my dad did show me that the Christian life was one of adventure. He showed me that following Jesus wasn't boring and predictable but a life laden with potential, looking for what God was up to and joining in.

I have two daughters, now six and eight years old. I want them to discover that the best thing that they can do with their lives is follow Jesus – the miracle man, who challenged injustice, welcomed outcasts, loved compassionately, gave his life for us – and invites us to follow him. Research shows how important the early years are for inspiring faith in the next generation. Children are naturally disposed to believe in the unseen, the supernatural and a Creator God. We get to work with their natural curiosity about how the world operates.

When I read the Gospels, I love how Jesus creates special moments with his disciples. There are times when he takes them to one side to explain the meaning behind the stories he has been sharing. There are times when Jesus climbs mountains and takes boat trips with them to impart fresh revelation. Then there are meal times and barbecues on the beach where he teaches them about the Father.

This book of 52 faith adventures is based around the idea of creating some special moments with our children where we can share what we have learnt about God. The word 'adventure' can become a bit of a buzzword. I am not talking about travelling around the world, climbing Everest, or scuba-diving shipwrecks, but I want these moments to be exciting, out-of-the-norm experiences.

These adventures supplement the small everyday traditions that are also valuable, like taking my kids to the park on Saturday morning and going to a 'greasy spoon' for breakfast on the odd occasion.

Many of the adventures in this book I have done with my kids. Some I did with my dad, some have been etched in my memory from childhood Boy's Brigade activities and some I have drawn from other books. Of course they are not just for dads. They are for carers, grandads, godparents, mums, and all other intrepid adventurers. Use them as a springboard. Don't feel hemmed in by them, but take these ideas as a starting point – get creative, invent your own and see where your faith conversations go!

ANDY FROST

USING THIS BOOK

My hope is that this book will help you do three things.

1. Make memories
I often meet parents with older kids who tell me how quickly the years go and to make sure I enjoy every moment. Between laundry cycles, lost swimming goggles, and last-minute homework, we can live life on autopilot, constantly looking forward to the next stage of childhood when our children will be slightly more independent. But the time goes fast and we need to enjoy the moments that are presented to us today.

The ideas in this book have helped me get out of a rut and create space to enjoy my kids. The house isn't always tidy and the dishes aren't always done, but we have been able to make some important memories. Good memories help bond families together, and psychologists have found that if children have a bank of positive memories with those who love them, they are generally happier and healthier[1]. When you embark on these adventures, I'd encourage you to create a scrapbook, photo diary or blog to record what you get up to!

As you go about creating memories, don't think that because these ideas are about passing on faith that we need to be really serious all the time. These adventures should be fun! Whether you end up purposefully getting really muddy, singing silly songs as you meander in the woods, or doing one of the adventures in fancy dress, you will be creating a memory that will last.

2. Share your experience of God
Some of us will approach this resource with great excitement, eager to learn more about depositing the truths of God into our children's lives. Others of us may be struggling with doubts and questions right now, and yet we want our children to grasp something of a Christian worldview.

Whether we are full of faith or struggling right now, the good news is that God is committed to our children and our role is simply to sow seeds of faith. As Jesus said, 'My Father is the gardener' (John 15:1).

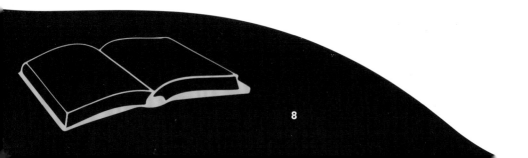

I have enjoyed weaving conversations about God into the ordinariness of life – telling Bible stories at bedtime, praying on the way to school, and talking through what we have just learnt as we drive home from church. But over the last few years, I have also loved taking my kids on lots of these mini adventures. It's often at these times that conversations about God become much more real. Each adventure is linked to a passage or story from the Bible, along with some possible questions and something you might like to pray about.

As we have talked about God, my daughters have frequently asked me questions that leave me flummoxed. Don't worry about having all the right answers or the perfect biblical knowledge. In these conversations, we don't need to have everything sorted – simply by talking about faith we are showing our children that we think the things of God are important.

3. Celebrate being a dad

I remember leaving the hospital ward when my first daughter was born. Becoming a father was a life-changing moment for me, and over the years I have learnt that it is both a huge privilege and a massive responsibility.

It's a privilege to watch our kids smile for the first time, take their first steps and try to tell their first joke. It's a responsibility to help our kids navigate friendships, encourage them to eat vegetables, and learn how to read their first book. Ultimately, how we parent will help shape how they will see the world.

As fathers, at times we can feel quite insecure. Sometimes I can feel that other dads have parenting nailed or that my wife is way more on top of things than I am. With work pressures, I know some men are worried they aren't stopping to enjoy the privilege of being a dad. Others I know are concerned about whether they are taking the responsibility of being a parent seriously enough.

From one dad to another, I want to say that you are doing a great job! We will not always get it right but we are playing a significant role in the lives of our kids. Whether you do one adventure from this book or all 52, remember to enjoy the ride.

[1] Chopik, William J. and Edelstein, Robin S. 2018, Retrospective Memories of Parental Care and Health From Mid- to Late Life. Published in the Health Psychology Journal of the American Psychological Association.

TIPS FOR INTREPID ADVENTURERS

1. You could do the adventures in order, but it may be more fun to flick through and see which ones take your fancy! They have been divided into four sections (see the Contents page) but please note that this is just meant as a guide – for example, not everyone will have a garden at home.

2. Most of the adventures are low-cost or free, and we have tried to give an idea of how much time and effort is needed for each one.

3. I'd strongly advise reading through the idea you are planning ahead of time. This will give you a chance to pray that God will bless your time and to make sure you have everything prepared!

4. Each adventure has a faith conversation linked to it, but please don't be limited by this. Use it as a springboard into your own ideas and thoughts and see where the conversations go. Ultimately it's not about trying to shoehorn lots of Bible knowledge into our children's heads, but rather creating opportunities for them to see the reality of a relationship with God.

5. If you haven't already, we'd really encourage you to get hold of a children's Bible to read along with some of these adventures. My favourite is the Jesus Storybook Bible by Sally Lloyd-Jones. You can read each story from your chosen children's Bible, but we've also included a short summary of each story or Bible verse, which you can use instead if you prefer. You might find that some of the discussion sections of these adventures will need to be adapted slightly to be age-appropriate for your children.

6. The activities in this book are aimed at children aged 3 to 11, but please use your own discretion. You know your kids best!

7. For those with more than one child, it is sometimes good to do an adventure with just one child at a time. This means you can have some quality one-to-one time together.

8. Sometimes our kids aren't in the mood for what we have planned. Feel free to go off the notes and be creative, especially when it comes to some of the discussion ideas. Some days it may be best to keep it to 30 seconds, and sometimes you might end up in a conversation about God for an hour! Don't feel pressurised, just enjoy seeing what your kids pick up on.

9. These are adventures for dads, but that doesn't mean you have to do them all in isolation! Why not do one of these adventures with another family? If Mum wants to come occasionally, then don't let her miss out. Research shows that faith is more likely to flourish when children feel that they belong to a wider family of God[2]. You could involve other significant adults in your children's lives, for example a grandparent, aunt, uncle, family friend, or someone from your church family.

10. Children with additional needs may not be able to join in with all these activities. Where you can, look for ways to adapt them to meet the needs of your child.

11. At the back of this book is a Bible overview that I put together for my children. In each adventure, alongside 'Bible to share', I have indicated which part of the Bible each story comes from, so that your child can see how the Bible fits together. For example, 'Bible Overview 6' would refer to the time of Jesus' ministry on earth as related in the four gospels.

12. The Bible does contain some difficult passages. It's important that your child is given space to ask questions. Personally, I find it helpful to always bring my children back to the person of Jesus. I also like using Rachel Turner's framework for discussion when we are posed with a hard question:

    i. Ask your child, 'What do you think?'
    ii. Share, 'Here's what I know.'
    iii. Share, 'Here's what I don't know.'
    iv. Then share, 'Here's how I live with that tension.'

TOP TIPS

[2] Powell, K.E. and Clark, C. 2011, Sticky Faith: Everyday Ideas to Build Lasting Faith in Your Kids. Zondervan.

SECTION 1

THE GREAT OUTDOORS

There's something special about the Great Outdoors. Whether it's a scenic mountaintop vista or a meandering trail sheltered from the swirling wind by a canopy of evergreens, being outside is good for the soul. In a world that is so screen-focused and filled with man-made structures, the wilderness reminds us that there is a Creator God who has given us the greatest of playgrounds to enjoy. In this first section are 13 adventures to take us out into the wilds beyond the comfort of our four walls.

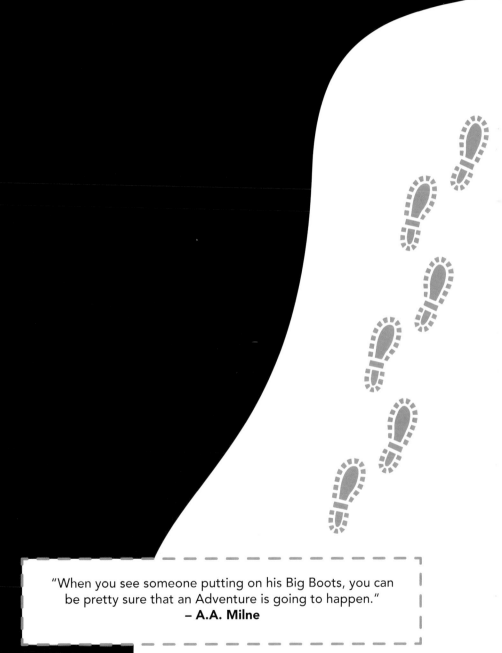

"When you see someone putting on his Big Boots, you can be pretty sure that an Adventure is going to happen."
– A.A. Milne

ADVENTURE 1
Stone Stacking

The art form of balancing rocks or stone stacking is common in many cultures and is done for a variety of different reasons. In the UK we often see heaps of stones called cairns that are used to mark out a route. But they are also often found as memorials or as part of a burial ground.

WHAT YOU DO:

1. Find a location that has plenty of rocks. Ideal places are riverbanks or beaches.

2. Collect some stones together and find a flat hard surface on which to build your stack. Show your child how to balance rocks on top of each other, building a mini stack. See how many stones they can stack on top of each other and how high they can take the stack without it toppling.

3. This activity helps children explore a range of concepts around the science of gravity, engineering and their artistic flair. Ask simple questions to help your child think about what they are doing.

4. Once they have mastered the stack, help model how they can counterbalance the rocks and stones to create arches and other gravity-defying stone structures. There are some great pictures online that you could show them to spark their enthusiasm – just search images for 'stone stacking' or 'rock balancing'.

5. With the stacking done, take a picture of your stones.

YOU COULD TRY THESE ...

BIBLE TO SHARE

JOSHUA 4:4-7 (Bible Overview 2)

Tell the story of the crossing of the Jordan.

In the days before Jesus, God's people, the Israelites, were travelling a long way to get to a new home that God had promised them. Led by a man named Joshua, they came to a big river which they needed to cross to get to their new home. They waited for three days and then, as the priests who were carrying a special box symbolising God's presence (the Ark of the Covenant) touched the water, the river stopped flowing. All the people crossed over safely. It was a miracle.

Joshua asked one person from each of the 12 tribes of Israel to carry a stone each from the riverbed to build a memorial. This was so that when Israelite children asked what these stones meant, their parents could tell them of the miracle when the river stopped flowing.

QUESTIONS TO ASK ...

What do you think it would have been like seeing the big river stop flowing?

Would you have been scared crossing the riverbed?

How big do you think the stones were that the 12 people chose?

What do you think the stone stack that God's people built would have looked like?

A THOUGHT TO PONDER

As you look at your stone stack with your child, think about God's faithfulness in your life. You might like to share one of those stories. Use simple and accessible language, such as 'God really helped me when ...'

LET'S PRAY

What can we be thankful to God for today?

TOP TIPS

Stack with care. Respect the environment and dismantle the stacks before you leave.

AGE RANGE: 3+
EFFORT LEVEL: 2/5
TIMING: 40 MINS (PLUS TRAVEL)
VITAL EQUIPMENT: SOME STONES

ADVENTURE 2

Night Hike

A night hike might sound quite 'out there' but with the sun setting early in the winter months in the UK, this could be an afternoon or early evening walk in the dark. Pack your torches and maybe a flask of hot chocolate for this mini adventure.

WHAT YOU DO:

1. Plan a route that is suitable for your child. Ideally, choose somewhere away from street lights and the noise of civilisation. The hike does not have to be far and could be a 25-minute loop or something more ambitious if your kids are a bit older.

2. Give a series of challenges during the walk. For example:
    - See how quietly you can walk for two minutes.
    - See who can do the best wild animal impression.
    - Have a go at making finger animals with the light from the torch.

3. During the walk, stop for a few minutes.
    - Be quiet and listen. What can you hear?
    - Turn off your torches. Give your eyes time to grow accustomed to the dark. What can you see?
    - Close your eyes, what can you smell?

4. Keep walking. Talk about what it's like walking in the dark. These questions might help:
    - What's the difference between walking in the day and at night?
    - How does it make you feel when we stand here in the dark?
    - Why are some people scared of the dark?

5. Stop again, turn off the torches and light your candle. (Depending on the age of your child, they may be able to hold their own candle.) As you look at the candle, share the Bible verse.

BIBLE TO SHARE

JOHN 8:12 (Bible Overview 6)

Jesus said: 'I am the light of the world. Whoever follows me will never walk in darkness, but will have the light of life.'

You could have a go at memorising this verse together.

QUESTIONS TO ASK ...

What do you think Jesus meant by this?

How does light help us live our lives?

What are some of the scariest situations we face?

How can knowing that Jesus is the light help us in them?

A THOUGHT TO PONDER

Light is essential for plants to grow. How does Jesus, the light of the world, help us grow? You might like to think about the fruit of the Spirit (Galatians 5).

Where there is light, there can be no darkness. As we walk with Jesus, we get to show his light in the world.

LET'S PRAY

As your child gets home and gets into bed, bring out the candle again, light it in the darkness and say a short prayer together, thanking Jesus that we don't have to be afraid of the dark because he is the light of the world.

You might like to set the scene as you embark on your hike, perhaps packing a teddy and some emergency supplies!

Make sure the terrain isn't too rough for your child when they are walking in the dark.

TOP TIPS

AGE RANGE: 4+
EFFORT LEVEL: 2/5
TIMING: 30-60 MINS
(PLUS 20 MINS PREP TIME)
VITAL EQUIPMENT: CANDLE, TORCH

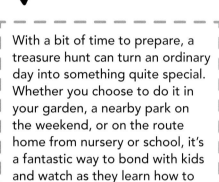

ADVENTURE 3

Lost Treasure

With a bit of time to prepare, a treasure hunt can turn an ordinary day into something quite special. Whether you choose to do it in your garden, a nearby park on the weekend, or on the route home from nursery or school, it's a fantastic way to bond with kids and watch as they learn how to work things out!

WHAT YOU DO:

1. In advance, choose the location to hide the treasure. The treasure could be a packet of popcorn or perhaps some glow sticks. You might want to wrap them up in a bin liner to keep them hidden from others.

2. Walk around the area where you are doing the treasure hunt, looking out for features such as bins, trees, street signs and fences.

3. Working your route backwards from the treasure location, write down a clue for the next location they will have to find. For example:

   'I have more letters than the alphabet' could be a postbox.
   'This is where you score a goal' could be a goalpost.
   'I am blue and made of metal' could be a fence.
   'The entry to friendship' could be the gate of a friend's home.

   The clue can be written down on a piece of paper and taped down at the previous location using sticky tape.

   If your child is getting a bit older, you could add a compass and begin each clue with a line such as, 'The next clue is west of where you are …' so that they can learn how to use a compass.

4. Eight to twelve clues is normally ideal and you will have to adapt the clues according to the age and ability of the children who are on the hunt.

5. When you are ready, hand your child the first clue and watch as they try to look for the hidden treasure.

6. When you find the treasure, you might want to talk about the following:
   - How hard was it to find the treasure?
   - What stories do you know about treasure?
   - What would be the best kind of treasure to find?
   - What makes treasure precious?

BIBLE TO SHARE
LUKE 15:8-10 (Bible Overview 6)

Tell the story of the lost coin.

Jesus tells three stories in quick succession about lost things (the lost sheep, the lost son and the lost coin). In this story, a lady has lost her precious coin.

The coin would have been worth a lot – maybe a day's wages. Aside from being valuable, the lady may have been fond of it in much the same way as we are fond of our favourite things. Jewish custom at the time was that a woman who got married took ten silver coins and sewed them into a headdress, and it could have been one of these that she lost.

First the woman lit a lamp. Then she swept up. This would have been a big job as the floor was probably covered in straw to make the floor softer underfoot. This was a big tidy-up. Then she searched until she found the coin.

When she found it she celebrated, inviting her friends round to celebrate too.

CONTINUED →

QUESTIONS TO ASK ...

How do we feel when we lose things?

How do we feel when we find things that were lost?

How might we be like lost treasure to God?

How do you think God celebrates when we choose to accept his love?

AGE RANGE: 3+
EFFORT LEVEL: 3/5
TIMING: 20-40 MINS
(PLUS 20 MINS PREP TIME)
VITAL EQUIPMENT: PEN AND PAPER
STICKY TAPE, COMPASS (OPTIONAL)

A THOUGHT TO PONDER

The celebration in this story is huge! This is how God celebrates over us when we choose to be with him. That's because we are precious to him.

You might like to share an experience of how you have felt lost, but how God has pursued you because he loves you. For example: 'When this happened, I felt … but God did this …'

LET'S PRAY

Let's ask God that we would know how precious we are to him.

Make sure you pick up all the clues and tape.

If it's raining, you can always set up a treasure hunt inside the house with clues like:
'I like to clean things' could be the washing machine.
'I have hands and a face but no body' could be a clock.

ADVENTURE 4

Camouflage

Kids love playing hide and seek but aren't always the best at it! This is your opportunity to coach your child to be a stealth ninja!

WHAT YOU DO:

1. You might like to begin by talking through the idea of camouflage. You could show them some pictures in an encyclopedia or online of animals that use camouflage to hide from prey. The Armed Forces often talk about eight words beginning with 'S' that are important to consider when hiding. You might like to talk them through with your child.

   Shade (colours, tones and patterns)
   Shine (things that are reflective)
   Shape (the shape of a person is easily spotted!)
   Shadow (casting shadows)
   Spacing (if there's a few of you hiding, don't space yourselves evenly)
   Silhouette (some local vegetation can disguise your head)
   Sudden movement (the eye detects speed)
   Sound (whispers!)

2. Find a path in a wooded area that has some bushes and trees on either side. Here's how the adventure works. Your child counts to 30 with their back turned to you, whilst you jog along the path. You have to hide on either side of the path but no more than five metres off the path. Note that it's a good idea to show your child how far five metres is beforehand.

CONTINUED →

3. Your child then follows up the path, walking and not running! If your child finds you, then they win but if they pass you, then you come out of your hiding place and inform them that they have lost!

4. You then switch round. You count for 30 seconds and your kids run up the path finding somewhere to hide.

As you take it in turns to hide, get them thinking about why people hide. These questions might help:
- Why do people hide?
- Where do you think is the best hiding place?
- What have you learned about hiding today?

BIBLE TO SHARE
ACTS 9:23-25 (Bible Overview 7)

Tell the story of Paul leaving Damascus.

Paul, a follower of Jesus in the days after Jesus went back up to heaven, was talking to people about Jesus in a city called Damascus. This made some people who didn't believe in Jesus very angry, and they made plans to kill Paul. Paul's friends helped him escape at night, lowering him down in a basket from an opening in the city wall.

As he had to leave very quietly, his camouflage was the basket and the cover of night.

QUESTIONS TO ASK ...

How would you have felt being lowered from a high wall in a basket?

I wonder why some people didn't like hearing about Jesus?

How do you think God might have helped Paul at this time?

A THOUGHT TO PONDER

In some parts of the world today it is still difficult to be a Christian. Being a follower of Jesus is not always easy. You might like to share an experience you've had – perhaps doing the right thing rather than following the crowd?

LET'S PRAY

Pray for those who, like Paul, have to live out their faith when their lives are being threatened.

It's always good to let your kids know that when you shout, "Game over!" they must come out of any hiding place – just in case!

Depending on how much your kids get into it, you might like to revisit the idea of camouflage. You could use face paints and teach them how to cover themselves with twigs and leaves to disguise themselves.

TOP TIPS

AGE RANGE: 4+
EFFORT LEVEL: 3/5
TIMING: 20-40 MINS
(PLUS 30 MINS PREP TIME)
VITAL EQUIPMENT:
FACE PAINT (OPTIONAL)

23

ADVENTURE 5

Trail Blazer

This adventure is about setting up a route for your child to follow. You can use one of a number of natural resources to signpost the route. For example, you could use sticks to make arrows, little piles of stones, or chalk-drawn arrows.

WHAT YOU DO:

1. Mark out the route, with each marker ten metres from the one before it. Remember to place the markers in varied places. Some could be very obvious, but not all of them should be at eye level.

2. When working out the route, think about where is best to end it. The route doesn't have to be really long. I have done this on a 2km woodland route and also around my local housing estate in London.

3. As your child(ren) follow the route, encourage them to be looking all around for markers and enjoy watching them work out where the next marker is.

4. Let them lead the way. If they go off course, don't direct them immediately, but let them work out how to come back to the last marker and look around again for the next.

5. When your child has completed the trail, ask them to reflect on what they have done. These questions may help:

   Which markers were the easiest/hardest to find?
   What happened if you were moving too fast?
   How easy was it to get lost?

TOP TIPS

If your kids are a bit older or there is another adult at hand, then you could choose to take a ten-minute head start and make the trail as you go along, hiding at the end (perhaps behind a tree – or up a tree if you are more athletic!).

If you are doing this activity in the summer, it could end with a picnic or an ice cream.

BIBLE TO SHARE

JOHN 14:6 (Bible Overview 6)

Tell the story of Jesus saying to his disciples, 'I am the way, the truth, and the life.'

On his last night before he went to the cross, Jesus washed his disciple's feet and shared an important meal with his disciples. His disciples knew that he would leave them soon and they were sad. Jesus comforted them, explaining that he was going to get their places in heaven ready for them.

Thomas asked, 'Lord, we don't know where you are going, so how can we know the way?'

Jesus answered, 'I am the way and the truth and the life. No one comes to the Father except through me.'

QUESTIONS TO ASK ...

What do you think Jesus meant when he said 'I am the way?'

How do you think Jesus made it possible for us to know his father, God?

What do you think heaven will be like?

How do we follow the way of Jesus if we can't see him today?

A THOUGHT TO PONDER

Jesus doesn't tell us the way but he becomes the way, ultimately by dying for us and rising again.

LET'S PRAY

As we thank Jesus for becoming the way, we might want to respond with open hands, allowing God to use us to help other people know him.

AGE RANGE: 3+
EFFORT LEVEL: 3/5
TIMING: 40 MINS
(PLUS TRAVEL)
VITAL EQUIPMENT: CHALK, OR NATURAL ITEMS TO MARK THE ROUTE

ADVENTURE 6

Tree Climbing

Climbing trees is a staple for many children as they grow up. This is your opportunity to go climbing with them, so you can see how many trees they can climb and how high they can get!

WHAT YOU DO:

1. Before you go out on the hunt for trees to climb, make sure you're wearing appropriate clothing that allows maximum flexibility. Avoid baggy clothing or accessories that can get caught on branches, in particular necklaces. When climbing you might choose to go barefoot, but if not make sure your shoes have good traction.

2. Before you set out, check the weather forecast! Strong winds and rain will make tree climbing dangerous. Never climb in thunderstorms and when it gets really cold in the winter, trees can become more brittle.

3. In finding a suitable tree, go for ones with large, sturdy branches, preferably ones you can reach from the ground. If trees have any clear signs of damage such as dead branches or mushrooms near the base, then give them a miss! If you find that the tree you are climbing has loose bark and soft wood, it may not be as healthy as you think and it's probably best to find another.

4. Before you climb it might be useful to share the climbing 'three point rule' which is that you should always try and support yourself at three different points at all times. For example, two feet and a hand or one foot and two hands. Ideally, in free climbing, these three points of contact would all be on different parts of the tree.

   These tips may also be helpful:
   - Grip onto branches nearer the trunk where they are most sturdy.
   - Avoid dead branches which are much weaker and may snap.
   - Stay vertical where possible.
   - When climbing, keep your body as close to the trunk as you can.

5. When you find the perfect tree, you might need to model how to climb it for your kids first. They may also need a lift up to the lowest branch to get going. Encourage them to climb slowly as they start out and don't push them if they get scared.

6. When they start getting higher up the tree, remember that when the trunk becomes thin it may not be able to hold their weight.

BIBLE TO SHARE

LUKE 19:1-10 (Bible Overview 6)

Tell the story of Zacchaeus.

Jesus was passing through a town one day and everybody wanted to see him. A man called Zacchaeus also wanted to see Jesus but because he was short, he couldn't see Jesus over the crowd. So he climbed a tree to see Jesus as he passed by. When Jesus saw him, he said 'Zacchaeus, come down; I'd like to have tea with you today.' Everybody in the crowd began to grumble, because Zacchaeus was known as a dishonest man. But Zacchaeus stood up in front of the crowd and said, 'Lord, I will give half my possessions to the poor, and pay back anyone I have cheated four times the amount I took from them.'

Ask them, as you tell the story, to imagine that this is taking place in one of these trees. If your children are older, you may need to explain to them what a tax collector is, and that they were despised by the people of Israel because they were working for the occupying Romans.

You could try reading the story again whilst they are sitting up in a tree and ask them to imagine they are Zacchaeus.

QUESTIONS TO ASK ...

You might want to chat about these as you continue to climb trees!

What would it have been like to be in the crowd?

Imagine you were Zacchaeus. How would it feel if Jesus had called out your name?

I wonder why Jesus went to Zacchaeus' house for tea?

Zacchaeus' life is changed in the story. Are there any ways in which Jesus is changing our lives?

CONTINUED →

AGE RANGE: 3+
EFFORT LEVEL: 2/5
TIMING: 20-40 MINS
VITAL EQUIPMENT: CLIMBABLE TREES

A THOUGHT TO PONDER

Zacchaeus means 'righteous one', a name that Zacchaeus had failed to live up to. What expectations do our teachers, friends, and family have of us? What might Jesus say about these expectations?

LET'S PRAY

Zacchaeus is changed from a man who is greedy to a man of generosity. Maybe you could pray asking how you could be generous this week, or to whom?

Tree climbing can be dangerous. Check the tree is sturdy before you climb and don't let your child climb beyond their capability.

TOP TIPS

ADVENTURE
7
Mountaintop Experience

When my eldest turned six we headed to Pen y Fan in the Brecon Beacons. It was a great first mountain to climb at 886 metres high. In the winter it can get pretty tricky with poor visibility and snow, but in August it's very achievable. A positive mountain-climbing experience is a great boost for a kid's confidence and they'll probably remember it forever.

WHAT YOU DO:

1. Find the right mountain. The UK has a number of good mountains or big hills. Find one that is close to you with an engaging and achievable route. From when you first start making plans, involve your child, so they can see what goes into making an adventure. If you aren't sure which mountains are appropriate for your kids, then your local Tourist Information Centre or the National Trust will be able to help. They will also be able to advise how well paths are signposted in case your map-reading skills aren't quite up to scratch.

2. Once you've chosen your mountain, plan the route. Get your kids involved from the outset and don't call it walking but 'exploring' or 'adventuring', otherwise they might lose interest before you've started. Get an Ordnance Survey map to carefully plot the route and try to teach your child how a compass works before you go. Remember that reaching the summit is only half the battle; you'll have to descend the mountain as well!

3. Carry a rucksack and pack the right gear. As well as food and water, it's vital to carry a torch, compass, map, whistle, first aid kit, any essential medication and a mobile phone. A portable battery charger for your phone may also be useful, particularly on longer routes. I'd recommend packing a waterproof jacket, a warm layer, gloves and a hat as temperatures can drop quickly on mountaintops. If you're climbing in the summer, pack extra water, your sun hat, and extra sun cream, as there's little shade on most mountains.

CONTINUED →

4. Be safe. Check the weather forecast before you set off and if the weather deteriorates, turn back. Tell someone reliable about your plans, which route you're taking (and stick to it) and what time you expect to return, so they can raise the alarm if you don't make it back by your given time. Remember to let them know if your plans change at all.

5. When you start walking, give plenty of gentle encouragement and remember that your child has shorter legs than you. Take plenty of short breaks to rehydrate and celebrate each stop by looking how far you have come. Keep showing your kids on the map where they are and help them work out what some of the symbols mean.

6. Packs of dried fruit, Jelly Babies and Tic Tacs help as a reward for completing stages along the route and boosting morale. If you will be walking all or most of the day, a picnic lunch is a good idea.

7. Keep it fun. Sharing stories, singing songs and creating space for good conversation are all great ways to bond as you walk. When you reach the summit, make sure you get a picture. You could get it printed and framed for your child as a memento!

BIBLE TO SHARE
1 KINGS 19:11-13 (Bible Overview 4)

Tell the story of God speaking to Elijah on the mountaintop.

In the days before Jesus, God often spoke to his people, the Israelites, through various different people called prophets. A man named Elijah was one of these prophets. One day he went up to a mountaintop, because in that place, God was about to pass by. First, there was a great howling wind that shook the mountain, but God was not in the wind. Second, there was a great earthquake, but God was not in the earthquake. After the earthquake there was a fire, but God was not in the fire. After the fire came a gentle whisper. It was God, talking to Elijah. Elijah came out of the cave he had been hiding in to listen to it, pulling his cloak over his face as he did so.

You could read this story at the top of the mountain and ask your child to imagine the wind tearing the mountains apart, the earthquake and the fire, perhaps making sound effects for each of them.

QUESTIONS TO ASK ...

What do you think God's voice might sound like, if you could hear it?

How would you have felt if you were Elijah in this story?

I wonder why God spoke in a small voice?

Why do you think Elijah pulled his cloak over his face when he came out to listen to God?

What are some of the different ways we might hear God today?

A THOUGHT TO PONDER

There is a difference between hearing and listening. Stop and be quiet with your child for 30 seconds and listen. What sounds can you hear? Listening is an active process.

LET'S PRAY

Spend two minutes being quiet, looking out at the view. What might God want to say to you today? Share anything you feel.

Do make sure you do the necessary preparation before you embark on your mountain hike and if you can't make the mountain top, celebrate how far you got.

If you get the mountain-climbing bug, then you might like to explore doing a Mountain Skills course – try searching online for ones in your area.

TOP TIPS

AGE RANGE: 5+
EFFORT LEVEL: 5/5
TIMING: 180+ MINS
(PLUS 120+ MINS PREP TIME)
VITAL EQUIPMENT: SOME GOOD WALKING TRAINERS/BOOTS, SUITABLE CLOTHING AND WATERPROOFS, TORCH, COMPASS, MAP WHISTLE, FIRST AID KIT

ADVENTURE 8

Fire Starter

Nothing quite beats making a fire! I have loved introducing my kids to fires and all their many uses – providing warmth, protection from animals, light in the darkness, and a place to cook marshmallows!

WHAT YOU DO:

1. First off, you need to create a fire bed. The fire bed should be bare earth (not grass!). If you can't find bare earth, you will need to dig away any grass or vegetation. After you've cleared the area, it's time to make your bed with 8-10cm deep of dirt. You can also make a fire on the beach, digging your fire bed in the sand.

2. You'll need to gather three basic types of materials to build your campfire:

   Tinder. For example, dry leaves, dry bark, wood shavings, dry grass. All of these catch fire easily and burn fast. Remember, wet tinder will not burn, and you will probably need more than you think!

   Kindling. Small twigs and branches (about the width of a pencil) make good kindling, to create the heat necessary to start a proper fire. Again, it must be dry and you will probably need more than you think!

   Fuel wood. These are the bigger branches – ideally as wide as an adult's forearm. This is what keeps the fire hot and burning. It can be slightly damp but ideally will be dry.

   When collecting wood, tell your child that if it snaps and breaks easily that means it is dry. If it is green, it is damp and will create more smoke.

3. Then you need to lay the fire. The most common way is the 'teepee'. To do this, you need to place the tinder in the middle of the fire bed and then build a teepee with some of the smaller kindling above it. Make sure you leave an opening in your teepee on the side the wind is blowing, as this will make sure your fire gets the air it needs. Then create a larger teepee around your kindling teepee with your fuel wood.

4. You can then light your fire in one of two ways; either by placing a lit match under your tinder or by using a ferro rod (point 5). However, you may like to have a paraffin fire starting block as a backup option, especially if it's wet.

5. If you choose to use a ferro rod (ferrocerium fire steel rod), the tinder will need to be really dry. Something like dead grass, weeds or twine (or cotton wool) is ideal. If your child is going to have a go at this, make sure they are wearing leather gloves. Hold the rod at a forty-five degree angle next to the tinder. Hold the striker firmly with your other hand and pull the rod back with a slow and steady motion.

6. Once the fire has caught light, the teepee structure will eventually fall. You can then add more logs to the fire.

7. Take this opportunity to skewer some marshmallows on sticks and roast them over the fire. What you are going for is a nicely browned marshmallow, not one that is just burnt!

8. When you're finished with your fire, it must be put out thoroughly. Remember that putting out a fire takes longer than you think – allow at least twenty minutes. Sprinkle water over the embers, stirring them with a stick to ensure all the ashes get wet. When the steam and hissing noises stop, you're almost done. Finally, put the back of your hand near the ashes. If you still feel heat, keep adding water and stirring. Once it feels cool, you can leave.

BIBLE TO SHARE

EXODUS 3-4 (Bible Overview 2)

Tell the story of Moses encountering God at a burning bush. If your child has seen DreamWorks' The Prince of Egypt, you might like to refer to this.

A man called Moses, one of God's people, was living in the wilderness as a shepherd. The rest of God's people were at that time enslaved by the Egyptian Pharaoh, but God had a plan to save them. Moses was out with his sheep one day when he saw a bush that was on fire, but the bush did not burn up. So Moses went over to get a better look, and the voice of God called to him out of the bush: 'Moses, Moses!'

Moses said, 'Here I am.'

CONTINUED →

AGE RANGE: 4+
EFFORT LEVEL: 5/5
TIMING: 60-90 MINS
VITAL EQUIPMENT: MATCHES
FERROCERIUM FIRE STEEL ROD & SCRAPER
(THESE COST £10-£15), BUCKET OF WATER
BAG OF LARGE MARSHMALLOWS

God said to Moses, 'Take off your shoes, for the ground you are standing on is holy. Now, listen. I have heard the cry of my people who are slaves in Egypt, and I have a plan to bring them out to a good land where they can be free. I am sending you to Pharaoh to bring my people out of Egypt.' Moses said to God, 'Why me? I'm nobody important. I can't bring your people out of Egypt.'

God said, 'I will be with you.'

QUESTIONS TO ASK ...

God got Moses' attention by appearing in a burning bush.

How does God get our attention today?

I wonder why God appeared in a burning bush?

Moses had to take his shoes off because the ground was holy. What do you think holy means?

If God was to meet us in this fire, what do you think he would say to us?

A THOUGHT TO PONDER

God calls his name, 'Moses, Moses!' It's very easy to find our identity in our present situation (Moses was in the wilderness working as a shepherd) or our past (Moses had enjoyed a royal upbringing and had fled Egypt as a murderer). But in this passage, Moses finds out who he is in his relationship to God. God knows our names and wants us to be in relationship with him.

LET'S PRAY

Think about how God is holy, how he is perfect. Say a prayer of 'wow', expressing your amazement at God's holiness. Then thank God that though he is perfect, he knows us by name and loves us.

Think about safety first. If you're camping and your site has a designated area for fires, use it. Always select a site at least a few metres away from buildings, trees, and other plants.

Keep a bucket of water nearby at all times. If the fire is not on your own property then make sure you leave the site of the fire as you found it.

ADVENTURE 9

Scavenger Hunt

This is an opportunity to get your child to explore a natural habitat, get muddy and see what they can find! A scavenger hunt begins with a list of things to find within a time limit.

WHAT YOU DO:

1. Find an outdoor location and set up a small piece of tarpaulin or a plastic box on the floor on which to place the things you have found.

2. Give your child a pre-written list of things to find. According to age and season, this list could include things like:

   A feather, a black stone, a conker, brown leaves, an acorn, five blades of grass, a pinecone, some thorns, an insect, something wet, something smooth, something rough, a really small rock, some moss, something yellow, some litter (which you then take home)!

   Alternatively, you may like to make a list around size, colour, texture and function such as:

   Find three things that are as big as your hand. Find six different things that are brown. Find two things that are prickly and three things that are soft. Find something that can be planted.

3. The aim is that the child brings each item and places it on the tarpaulin or in the box within a certain time limit. If you have more than one child, you might like to make it a competition. Or they could be competing against you!

4. Once you have collected all the items, spend some time looking at the intricacy of what you have found – the markings on a stone and the smell of the grass. What is the favourite thing you have found?

CONTINUED →

BIBLE TO SHARE
MATTHEW 6:26-29 (Bible Overview 6)

Jesus explained to his followers that they did not need to worry, because God cares for and provides for them. He said, 'There is far more to your life than food or clothes. Look at the birds – they don't worry about a thing, and yet God feeds them. And the flowers – they don't worry about how they're dressed. You are far more valuable to God than birds and flowers.'

Jesus was encouraging his followers to realise that worry was the wrong priority – it was about focusing on their needs, rather than focusing on God. Jesus makes it clear that God provides. Birds were often thought of as the least of God's creation (as shown in their worth in the sacrificial system) and dry grass was often just used to heat the oven, yet God looks after them.

Ask your child to picture the scene as Jesus is on a hillside teaching the people. Explain how Jesus used things in nature to teach us about life.

QUESTIONS TO ASK ...

Do you think birds use fridges and freezers to store their food?

Do you think birds and flowers worry?

What do we need in life?

What should we do when we feel worried?

Why can we trust God?

☑ feather
☑ a black stone
☐ a conker
☐ brown leaves
☑ an acorn
☐ 5 blades of grass

A THOUGHT TO PONDER

In this passage, Jesus recognises that we all need clothes, food and drink. In Jesus' time, there was no local supermarket and people often worried about how to meet these needs. Jesus told them not to worry. He says that we are more precious than birds and flowers. Jesus tells us that we can give our worries to him. What might we be worried about?

LET'S PRAY

Thank God for his creation. You might like to keep your eyes open and see how many different things you can thank him for. Give him any of the worries we might have and ask him that he would help us trust him.

There are a number of scavenger hunt PDFs that you can download and print online.

A clipboard and a pen for your child may be helpful, so they can tick things off.

TOP TIPS

Explain the rules before you hand out the list or it will be difficult keeping their attention. It might be a good idea to remind your child not to eat anything – particularly wild berries and mushrooms – and point out any plants that you know are dangerous (perhaps with the help of a plant identification field guide book).

Put what you have found back in the wilderness.

AGE RANGE: 3+
EFFORT LEVEL: 3/5
TIMING: 40 MINS (PLUS TRAVEL)
VITAL EQUIPMENT: TARPAULIN OR PLASTIC BOX, PAPER WITH SCAVENGER LIST CLIPBOARD AND PEN (OPTIONAL)

ADVENTURE 10

Dam Building

I used to love building dams as a kid. There is something special about wading through water trying to think through how best to stem the flow using natural resources. Dam-building helps teach kids basic engineering principles and about controlling water flow, as well as being great fun!

WHAT YOU DO:

1. The first thing is to find a stream. This might be the trickiest bit and it could well be worth finding one before you set off with kids in tow.

2. When you find your stream, find where you want to build the dam. It could be at the narrowest point or where it's most accessible for your kids.

3. Get your kids to run with their ideas as they try to stop the water flow.

4. Rocks are generally the best natural resource to use first, and it's normally best to start building the dam from one side. If there are no rocks around, you will need to use branches and logs.

5. Remember to start with the bigger rocks and logs and then use the small ones. You might like to use mud to fill in any of the gaps.

6. Having finished your enterprise, enjoy your accomplishment and talk through what might happen if the dam remained up permanently. What might happen to animals, the trees and the plants downstream?

7. Now demolish the dam, making as much noise as you can! Remember to put the rocks and logs back where you found them. Probably time to get dry!

BIBLE TO SHARE

PSALM 1:3 (Bible Overview 3)

Psalm 1:3 describes someone who is blessed as being like 'a tree planted by streams of water, which yields its fruit in season and whose leaf does not wither'.

QUESTIONS TO ASK ...

What is your favourite fruit?

How might people have fruit in their lives? You might like to think about the fruit of the Spirit (Galatians 5).

In the same way that trees need water, what do we need?

How can we plant ourselves near God to flourish?

A THOUGHT TO PONDER

Seeds can't choose where they are planted, but we can. Psalm 1 gives some wisdom about how we should position ourselves by delighting in the law of God. Dwelling on God's truth and love will help us become rooted in our relationship with him.

LET'S PRAY

Take a moment to be quiet and to ask God that, as a tree knows it needs water, we would know God's love.

TOP TIPS

Make sure you destroy the dam before you leave! Changing water flow can be extremely damaging to natural habitats.

AGE RANGE: 5+
EFFORT LEVEL: 5/5
TIMING: 60-90MINS
(PLUS PROBABLE TRAVEL TIME)
VITAL EQUIPMENT: A SHALLOW STREAM
WELLIES AND DRY CLOTHES
PLUS A COUPLE OF OLD TOWELS

ADVENTURE 11
Newspaper Kites

Kites are super-popular with kids. You can buy some amazing power kites, but if you're taking your child out for an adventure, then why not make your own kite? If you go online there are a whole range of ways of doing so, from using solely recycled material to making massive kites out of pieces of tarp. It might well be worth watching a YouTube video on how to build a kite before you attempt it!

WHAT YOU DO:

1. We're going to make newspaper kites. Before you head out, you'll need to make the kite. First of all, assemble all the necessary components. You'll need bamboo sticks, a newspaper, kite string, scissors and some garden shears (or something that can cut bamboo sticks easily).

2. Take a full piece of newspaper and spread it out on the floor. You'll need one stick to be the length of the paper (the spine) and one the width of the paper (the spar). If your sticks are too long, ask your child where they need to be cut and use some garden shears to cut them.

    (Note that ideally you want a slightly sturdier stick for the width and one with a bit more give as the longer stick.)

3. Use some kite string to tie the two sticks together in the middle, making a cross shape.

4. With a knife, make a small slit in both ends of both bamboo sticks. Then take one long piece of kite string and feed it through the four slits, making the shape of the kite using the string. The string should be very tight and once it is, tie it at the end where you started, using masking tape to make sure it's secure.

5. Lay your kite skeleton on the piece of newspaper and then fold the corners over the string, using either glue or masking tape to stick them down.

6. You can get creative now and decorate the kite with paint or even add a tail with pieces of fabric. (Remember not to make the kite too heavy or too wet with paint!)

7. Finally, you need to string your kite. Go to one corner of your kite and poke two holes, one on each side of the bamboo stick, and about one inch in from the side of the kite. So that the paper does not tear, I tend to use a piece of masking tape and a skewer to make the holes. Thread a small piece of string through the two holes and tie a knot on the side that the bamboo sticks show. Repeat this for all four corners.

   Now tie a piece of string from the top loop to the bottom loop. Then tie another piece of string from one side loop to the other side loop. When doing this, remember to leave some slack so that the kite can fly well!

   Once these two pieces of string are in place, gather them both in the centre and attach them together using another piece of masking tape. You can then tie a good length of string (at least five metres) or the ball of kite string to the join.

8. With your kite ready, you're set to go and fly it!

BIBLE TO SHARE
JOHN 3:8 (Bible Overview 6)

Jesus is talking to an important religious man called Nicodemus about what it means to be born again as we choose to follow him. He uses the analogy of the wind to describe the work of the Holy Spirit.

The Message Bible puts it like this: 'You know well enough how the wind blows this way and that. You hear it rustling through the trees, but you have no idea where it comes from or where it's headed next. That's the way it is with everyone 'born from above' by the wind of God, the Spirit of God.'

CONTINUED →

AGE RANGE: 4+
EFFORT LEVEL: 4/5
TIMING: 60-90 MINS
VITAL EQUIPMENT: BAMBOO STICKS (PLEASE NOTE THAT THESE ARE THE GARDENING VARIETY – THE FOOD SKEWERS ARE TOO SHORT. MAKE SURE THE STICKS ARE THIN OR THEY WILL BE TOO HEAVY YOU COULD ALSO TRY TO FIND YOUR OWN!), A NEWSPAPER, KITE STRING, MASKING TAPE, SCISSORS AND SOME GARDEN SHEARS

QUESTIONS TO ASK ...

What do you think wind would look like if you could see it?

Are there other things that we can't see that are powerful?

I wonder how the Holy Spirit is like wind?

What do you think happens when we invite God's Spirit into our lives?

A THOUGHT TO PONDER

Lie down on the floor and look up at the sky.

If there are clouds, how fast are they moving? What shapes can you see? (If there are different types of clouds and your child is old enough, you could go through the different types of clouds. If you're not sure, have a quick Google search first!)

If there are no clouds, look to the vegetation and see how it is affected by the wind.

How has God affected you? You might like to share first, and then encourage your kids to do the same.

LET'S PRAY

Stand up in the wind again, and feel it on your face and blowing your hair.

Pray something like, 'Holy Spirit, we invite you into our lives. Show us your power and your love and refresh us today.'

If there is no one around, you might like to shout the prayer.

Afterwards, you might like to see if as you prayed, you felt God at all.

Be careful with the garden shears and don't let young children cut the bamboo sticks.

Never fasten a kite to yourself and never use electric wire. Never fly kites near power lines or around other people.

TOP TIPS

ADVENTURE 12
Obstacle Course

My kids love a good obstacle course. I have done them in parks creating a circuit which involves climbing up and down the climbing frames and shooting down slides, and I have done them in the house jumping off the couch and balancing along the bench. But nothing beats an obstacle course in the great outdoors!

WHAT YOU DO:

1. Find a location for your assault course and work out a route. I tend to find that five to seven obstacles are ideal and the route can be circular or linear. Depending on the ages of your children, it may be as short as 25 metres or as long as a kilometre! Use the natural undulations of the area you are in to make the course as fun as possible. You might like to mark the course out with little piles of flour or sawdust. Here's a list of some of my favourite obstacles that you can set up:

   Spider's Web: Take a ball of string and thread it back and forth between two trees, both high and low. When your child comes to this obstacle, they have to climb through the gaps but they must not touch the string or they risk getting a ten-second addition to their time.

   Balancing Bar: Try to find a fallen tree or log that they walk across without falling.

   Ball Throw: Set up five plastic cups on a tree stump and mark out a throwing line with a ball placed on it. At this obstacle they need to pick up the ball and knock down the plastic cups. Each time they miss or knock one down, they need to retrieve the ball, head back to the line, and throw again. They can only move on when all five cups are knocked down.

   Under Tarp: Set up a piece of tarp using trees or sticks that they must crawl under.

CONTINUED →

The Run Around: Using cones or trees, mark the route so that it weaves around objects.

Jumping Crosses: Use a stick to mark the ground with a number of crosses (between five and eight). Your child needs to jump from one to the next as they go round the route.

Water Carry: Add a bucket of water that they have to carry for a section of the course which they have to try not to spill.

On the Line: Lay a long piece of string or rope on the floor for a section of the course that they have to have their feet on the whole time, or else they get a time addition!

2. Mark out the start line and the finish line.

3. Once the course is set up, it's best to walk your child around the course explaining what needs to be done at each section.

4. When they're ready, pull out the stopwatch and see how fast they can make it round the course. My kids often like to do the course three or four times to see if they can better their time.

5. If the course is too hard or too easy, then adapt it as you need to. And why not give it a go yourself whilst your child takes charge of the timer!

BIBLE TO SHARE
EXODUS 16:1-5 (Bible Overview 2)

Moses has led God's people, the Israelites, out of Egypt. They are in the wilderness and the people are facing various obstacles – such as the need for water to drink and food to eat. They begin to think back about the meat they could eat in captivity and keep grumbling!

In this short extract from the Exodus story, God miraculously provides food called manna for them to eat. Later on in the chapter, he also provides small birds called quail for them to eat too.

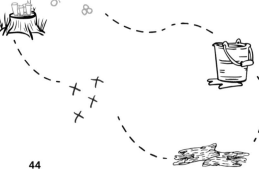

QUESTIONS TO ASK ...

The people of God had been miraculously rescued from Egypt with the plagues and the route through the Red Sea, and yet they kept grumbling. What are some of the things we grumble about?

What do you think it would have been like to wander around the desert for 40 years?

Do we ever grumble to God? What do you think God might say to us?

A THOUGHT TO PONDER

The Israelites kept focusing on the issues they were facing rather than bringing the issues direct to God. What happens when we take our attention from the obstacles and remember the character of God?

LET'S PRAY

Think about which obstacle or challenges we might be facing in life. Then go through the alphabet from A to Z trying to think of a different word to describe God for each letter. Spend a moment asking God to help us keep our eyes on him and not on the obstacles.

When doing obstacle courses, it can be good to take a first aid kit with you, just in case there is a grazed knee.

Also as you walk through the course, do look out for any hazards (such as tree roots and stinging nettles) and point them out to your child.

TOP TIPS

AGE RANGE: 5+
EFFORT LEVEL: 4/5
TIMING: 30-60 MINS
VITAL EQUIPMENT: STRING, TARP, CONES BUCKET AND WATER, PLASTIC CUPS AND BALL(S), FIRST AID KIT

ADVENTURE 13
Lakeside

The UK has over 40,000 lakes, so there should be one within reach of your home. Find one that you can visit to build a mini den and have a picnic, thinking about one of those classic stories that we find in the Gospels.

WHAT YOU DO:

1. Travel to a nearby lake, taking with you two sheets of tarpaulin, a long ball of string (or washing line) and some pegs.

2. Find somewhere quiet around the edge of the lake to build your temporary base. You will need two trees that are at least ten feet apart and ideally flat land between them.

3. To build your den, tie the string to the two trees about five feet from the ground, making it taut. Then drape one piece of tarpaulin over the string, using the pegs to secure it to the string. Spread the edges of the tarpaulin out, using rocks or wood (or tent pegs) to hold it in place. Depending on your child's capabilities, you could ask them to do some of the den set-up themselves!

4. Put the other piece of tarpaulin down as a ground mat under the erected tarpaulin to keep you from getting wet and muddy.

5. Time for the picnic! But before you dig in, bring out the five 'loaves' (it could be small individual buns or baguettes) and the tin of fish (it could be tuna or sardines) and share the story below.

BIBLE TO SHARE

JOHN 6:1-14 (Bible Overview 6)

Jesus was teaching a huge crowd of people by the side of a lake. It was late in the day, and no-one had any food to eat. Jesus asked his disciples, 'How should we feed these people?' One of the disciples said, 'There's a little boy here who has five barley loaves and two fish. But that will never feed everybody.'

Jesus took the bread and fish and, giving thanks to God, broke them and gave them out to the crowd. There was enough for everybody with plenty of leftovers – even with over 5,000 people there!

Ask your child to imagine that this story is happening here. Now hand them the five pieces of bread and the tin of fish.

QUESTIONS TO ASK ...

How do you feel when you are really hungry?

I wonder why the boy offered his lunch to help feed the crowd?

How would you have felt if Jesus gave you a few pieces of bread and some fish to feed so many people?

How would you have felt about Jesus after the miracle?

A THOUGHT TO PONDER

God gives each of us gifts, skills, and talents that we can use for him. What gifts, skills and talents do you have? The bread and fish might not have looked like much, and yet God did something incredible with them. What have we got to offer to God today?

LET'S PRAY

The miracle was done after Jesus prayed a prayer of thanks. Before you tuck into your picnic, stop and be quiet for a moment, looking at the lake and then thank God for your feast.

Always be careful near open water. Do make sure that your child does not go to the water's edge alone and keep your eyes on them the whole time!

TOP TIPS

AGE RANGE: 3+
EFFORT LEVEL: 3/5
TIMING: 60-90 MINS (PLUS TRAVEL)
VITAL EQUIPMENT: TWO SHEETS OF TARPAULIN (IDEALLY ONE SHOULD BE 15 FEET SQUARED), ONE LONG BALL OF STRING OR A WASHING LINE, SOME WASHING LINE PEGS, PICNIC (INCLUDING FIVE SMALL LOAVES AND A TIN OF FISH) TIN OPENER, SOME TENT PEGS (OPTIONAL)

SECTION 2

SEASONAL ADVENTURES

There is a natural rhythm to the year. The moon and the sun mark the months and years, the weather and the vegetation mark the seasons. On top of the natural flow to God's creation, we also have the Christian calendar with its depth of tradition and heritage that allows us to explore more of God as we journey through the year. Mark some key moments in the year by reflecting on important events in the calendar and creating some mini adventures to go with them.

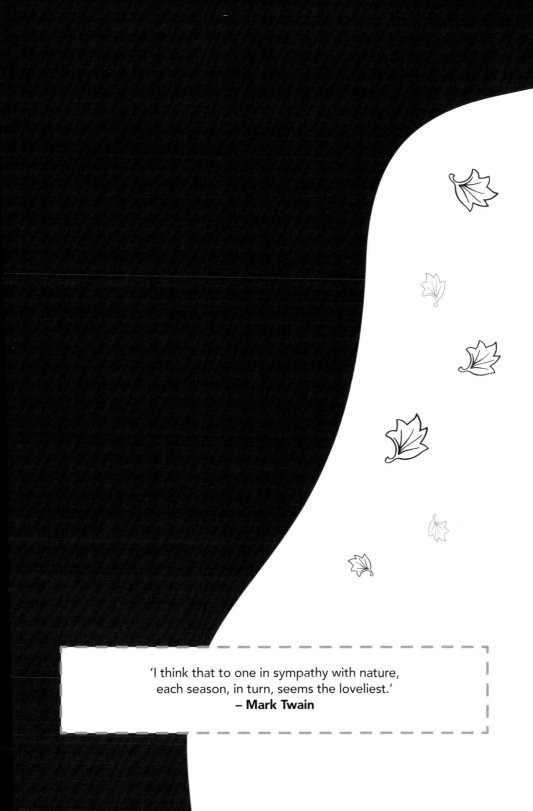

'I think that to one in sympathy with nature,
each season, in turn, seems the loveliest.'
– Mark Twain

ADVENTURE 14

New Year's Day Pooh Sticks

1st JANUARY

New Year is always an opportunity to reflect on the year that has been and think about the year ahead. As children get older they become able to reflect on longer periods of time. This adventure is an opportunity to help them reflect whilst playing the legendary 'Pooh sticks', which was first mentioned in a Winnie-the-Pooh book – hence the name!

WHAT YOU DO:

1. Find a bridge over moving water.

2. Hunt around the area for some sticks and twigs. We tend to find a few each of different length and size to try and ascertain what makes the perfect pooh stick.

3. Check which way the water is flowing and stand on the side of the bridge with the water flowing towards you.

4. Make sure everyone knows what their stick looks like. Then, on the count of three, everyone drops their pooh stick from the same height into the water below. (No throwing allowed!)

5. You then race to the other side of the bridge to see which stick appears first from underneath. We find that cheering for your stick often helps.

6. The winner is the owner of the stick that floats underneath the bridge fastest.

7. You can repeat this exercise with different sticks, looking closely at where the water is fastest flowing for the extra advantage.

TOP TIPS

If the bridge is high, be really careful and don't let your kids lean over too far when watching their stick, just in case they topple over!

BIBLE TO SHARE
1 THESSALONIANS 5:16-18 (Bible Overview 7)

Paul wrote this letter to the church in Thessalonica, in modern-day Greece. These verses say: 'Rejoice always, pray without ceasing, give thanks in all circumstances; for this is the will of God in Christ Jesus for you.'

QUESTIONS TO ASK ...

How do we pray without stopping?

In which situations is it hardest to pray to God?

What are we thankful to God for?

Why do you think God would want us to thank him?

A THOUGHT TO PONDER

Stand on the bridge with the water flowing away from you. As the water rushes away below, think about the last year and the time that has gone. What is there to be thankful to God for?

Move to the other side of the bridge with the water rushing toward you. What are some of your hopes and dreams for the year ahead? How can we pray into them?

LET'S PRAY

The Examen is an ancient way of reflecting prayerfully before bed, asking the question, 'Where has God been in the events of the day?' I find these five components helpful and often do it with my kids before bed but it can also work looking back at the year.

1. Be aware that God is present now. Thank him for the day (year) – what has been good?
2. Review the day (year) – where has God been present?
3. Think through the day (year) and how you have felt at different times.
4. If you have reacted wrongly in some way, say sorry to God.
5. Look forward to the next day (year) – how can God help you live well?

AGE RANGE: 3+
EFFORT LEVEL: 1/5
TIMING: 20 MINS
VITAL EQUIPMENT: STICKS AND A BRIDGE OVER MOVING WATER

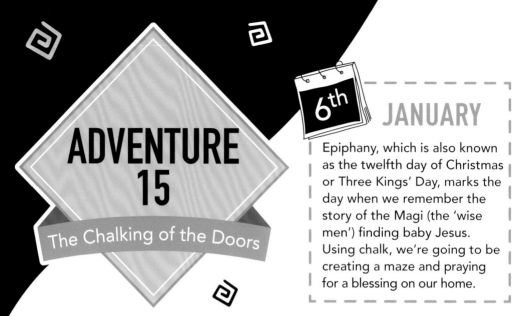

ADVENTURE 15

The Chalking of the Doors

6th JANUARY

Epiphany, which is also known as the twelfth day of Christmas or Three Kings' Day, marks the day when we remember the story of the Magi (the 'wise men') finding baby Jesus. Using chalk, we're going to be creating a maze and praying for a blessing on our home.

WHAT YOU DO:

1. Get some chalk and head out to find a big piece of concrete.

2. Draw a maze on the concrete. There are various templates online or you can get creative and make your own. Make the paths big enough to walk along. Ideally, you'd set this up beforehand.

3. Talk through how mazes work and see if they can walk through it without hitting a dead end! If your child is young, they may enjoy trying to push their toy cars around it. If your child is a bit older, and they find it too easy, then do the following:

   Blindfold your child and using the terms 'right', 'left', 'forward' and 'stop', see if they can walk the maze without touching the chalk outline. You could then blindfold yourself and see if they can guide you around the maze.

   If it's still easy, see if they can memorise the maze and then with a blindfold on, walk the route without looking!

BIBLE TO SHARE

MATTHEW 2:1-12 (Bible Overview 6)

Christmas might already seem like a while ago, but retell the story of the Magi. We are not sure exactly how long after Jesus' birth the Magi arrived, but it may have been as long as two years. When Jesus was born, three wise men from the East saw the light of the star over Bethlehem and travelled to worship Jesus.

On the way, they stopped to ask King Herod, the king of Israel at the time, where they could find 'the new king of the Jews', by which they meant Jesus.

Herod was a bad man, who was worried that a new king would replace him. He said to the wise men, 'Go and find this child, and then report back to me.' So they went on to Bethlehem and found Jesus, presenting their gifts of gold, frankincense, and myrrh. But they were warned by God in a dream not to go back to Herod, so they went home by a different route.

QUESTIONS TO ASK ...

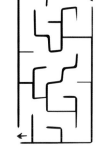

What was the trickiest thing about the maze?

What do you think made the journey for the wise men tricky?

What would you have brought Jesus as a gift?

A THOUGHT TO PONDER

There is a Christian tradition called 'chalking the doors' where you write the following formula above the door of your house using chalk:

20 + C + M + B + 22

The '20' at the beginning and the two digits at the end mark the year (i.e. the formula above would be for 2022).

The letters stand for the initials of the Magi: Caspar, Malchior, and Balthazar. (These are not found in the Bible.)

But they also stand for the abbreviation of the Latin phrase Christus mansionem benedicat which simply means, 'May Christ bless the house'.

The '+' signs represent the cross.

LET'S PRAY

Think about the times you will have in your house over the year – eating, resting, playing, reading ... and the people who might visit. Then ask God's blessing on your home.

TOP TIPS

Why not ask your child to create their own maze for you to try to master?

Although the chalk will wash away with the rain, if you are using a public place it's probably a good idea to pour some water on the chalk and give it a quick brush away.

AGE RANGE: 3-6
EFFORT LEVEL: 4/5
TIMING: 20-50 MINS
VITAL EQUIPMENT: CHALK, A BLINDFOLD A BRUSH AND BUCKET OF WATER

ADVENTURE 16
Pancake Race

SHROVE TUESDAY & ASH WEDNESDAY

'Pancake Day', as it has become affectionately known, is the day before Lent begins. You may have heard about the idea of a pancake race, which is thought to have originated in Buckinghamshire and has been running since 1445. This adventure takes your pancake tossing out of the front door!

WHAT YOU DO:

1. First up, you need to make some pancake batter. If there are two of you, this should work:
   100g plain flour
   2 large eggs
   300ml milk
   1 tablespoon of sunflower or vegetable oil
   Pinch of salt

2. When thoroughly mixed, leave the batter to chill for 30 minutes (if possible).

3. Get out the frying pan and give the inside a quick wipe with some oiled kitchen paper. Then get a medium heat going.

4. Cook your pancakes for one minute on each side. They should be golden coloured. To turn the pancakes, you can either use a spatula or try tossing it!

5. Now before you get to eat the pancake, try some pancake race challenges. Here are my top three!

   The Race – this is a race while tossing a pancake. Set out the length of the race. It could be once up the street or down the garden. If you have two pans, you can race each other, otherwise it will need to be a time trial with a stopwatch. The measure of success is how many times the pancake needs to be flipped whilst running! So decide on that before you start and give your child a chance to practice, to get used to tossing a pancake.

High Toss – how high can you get your pancake in the air before catching it?

Toss to Plate – when you toss the pancake, can your child catch it on a plate? (I recommend not using fine china!)

6. Finally, it's time to add some toppings. Caster sugar and lemon is the classic but you can obviously get very creative here! Can you even decorate the pancake to look like you? (Banana for the eyes, honey for the hair …)

BIBLE TO SHARE
GENESIS 3:19 (Bible Overview 1)

We are about to start Lent. Shrove Tuesday is a feast before people fast for Lent. The idea is that people think about how they might need to change their lives and how they can grow in their relationship with God. Ash Wednesday is the first day of Lent, when people often reflect on this verse.

In the creation story, God created man from the dust. (The name Adam actually means earthling or 'made of the earth'.) God breathed into his nostrils the breath of life and then he came to life. When Adam and Eve chose to rebel against God and put themselves at the centre of their story, the consequence was death. 'Remember that you are dust and to dust you shall return.'

QUESTIONS TO ASK ...

Why do you think Christians have both moments of feasting (with pancakes) and moments of being serious (like Ash Wednesday)?

What do you think it means to come from ash and to go back to ash?

I wonder why some people give things up for Lent?

Is there anything that you are going to give up for Lent?

CONTINUED →

AGE RANGE: 6+
EFFORT LEVEL: 3/5
TIMING: 20-40 MINS
VITAL EQUIPMENT: PANCAKE MIXTURE PAN, PEN AND PAPER, MATCHES METAL CONTAINER TO BURN PAPER IN

A THOUGHT TO PONDER

The ashes of Ash Wednesday symbolise death and repentance (which really means turning away from our selfishness and towards God). We remember that we will one day die and that none of us are perfect. As Christians we enter Lent solemnly, but also knowing that we are on the countdown to Easter to celebrate Jesus' victory over sin and death.

LET'S PRAY

In some church traditions, people mark their heads with ash on Ash Wednesday. Take a few moments to write down or draw some of the things that you are sorry for and then thank God that he forgives us. Then burn the paper to make some ash and mark the sign of the cross on each other's heads.

TOP TIPS

Pans get hot and so gloves may be a good idea for when you go pancake tossing.

ADVENTURE 17

Guerilla Gardening

SPRING

Guerilla Gardening is simply improving a neglected or overgrown public space by adding some plants. Some people do it under cover of darkness, so that in the morning people see the transformation, but you can do it at any time of the day.

WHAT YOU DO:

1. Find a neglected plot of land – it could be on the edge of a pavement, between buildings, or in front of a row of shops. A small piece of land is ideal and if you go online and search for 'Guerilla Gardening' you'll find a few examples.

2. Prepare the plot of land by removing weeds and rubbish. Try to discern what type of soil you have – is it clay-like or earthy?

3. Once you know what kind of soil you have, you need to decide what plants you want to use. The hope is that the plants will thrive and so here are a few tips when selecting what to plant:

   Choose plants that grow naturally in your location, as they will be better suited to the amount of sun and rainfall they will receive.

   Choose hardy plants that don't need lots of care and frequent watering.

   Choose plants that can flourish in the soil you have and in the conditions of your piece of land. For example, is your spot very shady?

   Choose cheaper plants, as your plot may be messed up by dogs or other kids with a football!

   Choose colourful plants that will make a difference visually to the area and get noticed.

CONTINUED →

4. Plan what you are going to do before you begin – even draw a little sketch with your child. Remember that spacing plants is important because as they grow, they spread out. (Most plants will have a spacing requirement on the plant tag.)

5. Before you plant, you might need to prepare the ground by turning over the soil and allowing it to aerate. When planting, dig a hole twice as wide as the plant's container, then take the plant out and set it into the ground. Replace the soil around the plant and add some water and fertiliser.

6. Clear away any rubbish and return when you can to water your eco-garden!

BIBLE TO SHARE
REVELATION 21:5 (Bible Overview 8)

The final book of the Bible is Revelation. It was written by John, one of the twelve disciples. Revelation shows how God's story ends as he makes everything new. Sin and evil will be done away with and a new heaven and new earth will be established. In this verse, John, in a vision, sees God on his throne declaring, 'I am making everything new!'

QUESTIONS TO ASK ...

How does the plot of land you have been working on look new?

How do you think the world will look different when God makes everything new?

What do you think needs to be made new in the world today?

I wonder why God doesn't just do it right now?

A THOUGHT TO PONDER

When talking of a new heaven and a new earth, John uses the Greek word kainos rather than the word neos. Neos means brand new, but kainos means made new or recycled. What does it mean to work with God in his plans to make things new?

LET'S PRAY

Jesus teaches us to pray to God the Father in this way: your kingdom come, your will be done.

As you head home from your plot, think about where you want to see God's kingdom come and his will being done, and pray for God to work in these situations.

The idea with guerrilla gardening is that you don't get permission. If this seems a bit too adventurous, then you could instead look around your street for a garden to revitalise and get permission to do it first.

Gloves are a good idea for your child, especially if there is rubbish there such as broken glass.

Why not take a 'before and after' photo to show the transformation?

TOP TIPS

AGE RANGE: 5+
EFFORT LEVEL: 5/5
TIMING: 90-120 MINS
(DEPENDING ON PLOT OF LAND AND DISTANCE FROM HOME)
VITAL EQUIPMENT: HOE, SPADE PLANTS, FERTILISER, WATER, GLOVES BIN LINERS (TO CLEAR AWAY ANY LITTER)

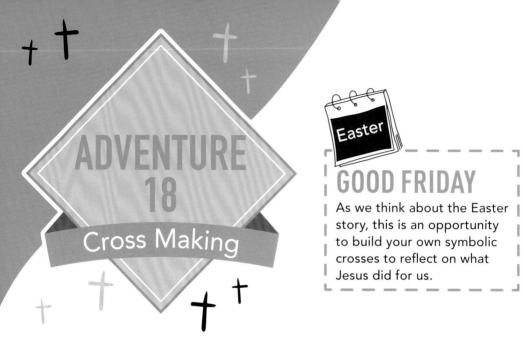

ADVENTURE 18

Cross Making

GOOD FRIDAY

As we think about the Easter story, this is an opportunity to build your own symbolic crosses to reflect on what Jesus did for us.

WHAT YOU DO:

1. There are two main components for making the cross: the string and the wood. You can make your own string (see points 2-4), or buy some string and skip this section!

2. To make your own string, you can purchase some raffia (which is often used for agricultural purposes to tie vegetables, plants in vineyards and floral arrangements) either online or from a garden centre. One packet will suffice unless you want to buy two different colours to make your string look fancy.

3. Take two strands of raffia and tie them together at the end. An overhand knot works well. Then pinch the knot between your left thumb and forefinger.

4. Using the other hand, pinch one of the two strands of raffia between your right thumb and forefinger and twist the raffia fibre away from you. As you twist, your forefinger will naturally go between the strands of fibre. Continue to hold the strand between thumb and forefinger and, placing the other strand between forefinger and middle finger, twist the entire bundle bringing the next strand up for twisting. Simply repeat this action over and over again to make the string. Once you have finished, tie a knot in the other end.

   This sounds pretty complicated as it is hard to explain in words! Do check out a video on YouTube if you can't quite grasp what to do.

5. Set out to a wooded area and on the way look out for the cross shape in paving stones, telegraph poles, street signs and fences.

6. When you arrive at your destination, search for two pieces of wood each – one that is longer than the other. Use the string to tie the two pieces of wood together to make a cross.

BIBLE TO SHARE
JOHN 3:16 (Bible Overview 6)

'For God so loved the world that he gave his one and only Son, that whoever believes in him shall not perish but have eternal life.'

Read or recite this, the most well-known Bible verse in the world. Keep repeating the verse, missing out one word at a time and see if your child can fill in the gap.

Then replace the phrase 'the world' with your child's name.

QUESTIONS TO ASK ...

What is the best way of showing love?

Why do you think Jesus died on a cross?

I wonder why we often have crosses up in our church buildings?

What does the cross mean to you?

A THOUGHT TO PONDER

At Easter, we remember how Jesus gave his life that we could be forgiven and know his love. We often take communion in church to remember what he did. In some countries, where the church has to meet secretly, they take communion with grapes. The skin and the juice remind them of the body of Jesus.

LET'S PRAY

Take a grape and eat it slowly. Thank God for his son Jesus and his obedience to God on the cross.

TOP TIPS

We can become overly familiar with the cross but when sharing with children, be aware that it might trigger some emotion.

AGE RANGE: 3+
EFFORT LEVEL: 4/5
TIMING: 20-40 MINS
(PLUS 20 MINS PREP TIME)
VITAL EQUIPMENT: STRING OR
RAFFIA STICKS, GRAPES

ADVENTURE 19
Egg Rolling

EASTER SUNDAY

The word Easter, and the idea of using eggs to celebrate it, are not found in the Bible. They date back to pre-Christian traditions, but early Christians saw a connection between eggs and the message of life and decided to adopt them into celebrating the resurrection. Egg rolling is an Easter activity that supposedly symbolises the stone in front of the tomb being rolled away. So let's try it!

WHAT YOU DO:

1. Boil some eggs. (I would recommend two each.)

2. Decorate your eggs with paint – ideally acrylic paint or oil-based paint. (This is to make sure you know whose egg is whose.) Once you've let it dry, cover the entire surface of each egg with glue to prevent the eggs from breaking.

3. Let the glue dry.

4. Now you have an option. You can either find a hill for your egg roll or you can build a course for your egg roll.

5. If you opt for a hill, then climb to a high point and sit down with your egg ready. You have to roll (not throw!) your egg and see how far it travels. The winner is the egg that goes the furthest. You can now try it on different parts of the hill with different gradients.

6. If you opt for a course, then you will need to find an open space, ideally a garden lawn with recently mowed grass. Mark out the race lanes. You can do this by finding twigs and sticking them in the ground and then attaching string or a ball of wool around the twigs. You will need a race line each for you and your child and the length of the track should be suitable for the capabilities of your child. To move the egg, tradition has it that you use a wooden spoon – definitely no hands! The starting position is kneeling at the starting line with the egg just in front. Have a referee (perhaps Mum!) call out, 'On your marks, get set, go' and then start pushing the egg round the course. (Note that you are not allowed to hit the other person's egg!) The winner is the first egg to cross the finish line.

BIBLE TO SHARE

LUKE 24:1-12 (Bible Overview 6)

After Jesus had died on the cross, his body was buried in a tomb outside Jerusalem, where the entrance was sealed with a stone. It was customary for Jewish women to anoint a body with spices after death as part of saying goodbye. Some women who were followers of Jesus – Mary, Joanna, Mary Magdalene and some others – went to Jesus' tomb but found that the stone had been rolled away and two angels were there instead of Jesus' body. They said, 'Why do you look for the living amongst the dead? He is not here, he has risen.'

You could read the story two or three times imagining that you are the women who get to the tomb first and thinking about the emotions they must have experienced.

QUESTIONS TO ASK ...

I wonder why we associate eggs with Easter?

After Jesus rose from the dead, it later appears that he could walk through walls. So why did he bother moving the stone away?

How do you think the news of Jesus rising from the dead was received?

What do you think Jesus' resurrection means for us?

A THOUGHT TO PONDER

'They found the stone rolled away from the tomb …' is an important verse. The resurrection is one of the greatest arguments for why the Christian faith is true. The tomb would have been guarded by four Roman soldiers who could have been executed for losing a 'dead body'. The stone blocking the tomb would have been large and heavy. So heavy (probably the weight of a car) that levers were normally used to move them. The best explanation for the empty grave is that Jesus really did rise from the dead.

LET'S PRAY

Thank God that Jesus not only died but that he rose again, and this means that we have a hope now and for evermore.

TOP TIPS

It's worth telling your child not to become too attached to the egg they have decorated as it may well crack.

AGE RANGE: 3+
EFFORT LEVEL: 3/5
TIMING: 20-60 MINS
VITAL EQUIPMENT: AN EGG ACRYLIC OR OIL PAINTS PAINTBRUSHES, A HILL OR A LAWN WITH TWIGS AND WOOL

ADVENTURE 20
The Geyser Experiment

WHAT YOU DO:

1. First of all, you need to make a geyser tube. Use the packet of Mentos to roll a piece of construction paper into a cylinder shape around the sweets. The paper should fit snugly but should still be loose enough so that the packet can still fall out. Once the paper is in place, tape it up using a piece of duct tape. Now remove the packet of Mentos.

2. Find an outside area. The place needs to be flat, so that you can stand the Diet Coke bottle.

3. Unscrew the top from the Diet Coke bottle and using duct tape, fix the tube securely to the bottle opening so that you have made a funnel for the sweets to drop down.

4. Just above the tape by the opening, slide a toothpick through the paper, to create a stopper. The toothpick needs to be central in the tube and needs to pierce both sides.

5. Drop half a packet of the sweets (5-7 Mentos) into the top of the tube.

6. Then when everyone is ready to watch, pull the toothpick out and run away!

7. If it's gone according to plan, just a few seconds later, you should now be watching a huge geyser of Diet Coke flying out of the bottle.

8. The science behind it? The carbon dioxide gas (that makes the bubbles) in the Diet Coke is wanting to escape. Mentos, when dropped into the Diet Coke act as surfactants that lower the surface tension between a liquid and a solid. The sweets are rough (and therefore have a larger surface area) and they sink to the bottom, thus having a greater impact.

BIBLE TO SHARE

ACTS 2:1-4 (Bible Overview 7)

After Jesus had risen from the dead and gone back to heaven, the disciples were all together praying in one place. Suddenly a noise like a rushing wind came from heaven and filled the whole house. They saw what looked like tongues of fire hovering over each person. Then they were all filled with the Holy Spirit and began to speak different languages by the power the Spirit gave them.

The term Pentecost comes from the Hebrew term 'shavuot' which means seven weeks. It marks the 50th day after the Passover. 50 days after the first Passover the wandering Israelite tribe had arrived at Mount Sinai. Moses came down from the mountain top with the Law of God, to find the people worshipping a golden calf.

1,500 years later, the disciples were in an upper room having seen Jesus raised from the dead. On this occasion they don't receive the Law but the Holy Spirit. As Peter gets up to preach, anointed by the Spirit, 3,000 people respond to the message of good news and join the Jesus movement. Pentecost, is in its very essence, a celebration of new life.

QUESTIONS TO ASK ...

Did you realise how much power was in the Diet Coke?

The disciples were in the upper room praying. What adjectives (describing words) do you think of when we talk about prayer?

There is the sound of a violent wind. What do you reckon that was like?

There are tongues of fire that rest on their head. What do you think that was like?

Who do you think the Holy Spirit is?

CONTINUED →

AGE RANGE: 4+
EFFORT LEVEL: 2/5
TIMING: 20 MINS
VITAL EQUIPMENT: LARGE BOTTLE OF DIET COKE
ABOUT HALF A PACK OF MENTOS
DUCT TAPE, CONSTRUCTION PAPER
OLIVE OIL (OPTIONAL)

A THOUGHT TO PONDER

The Greek word dunamis refers to power and is the root word of our English word dynamite. In Acts 1:8 Jesus has told the disciples that they will receive dunamis (power) when the Holy Spirit comes to help the disciples share about the good news. In Acts 2 the Holy Spirit empowers the disciples to speak in other languages so that they can talk to people from different countries about Jesus. Is there an experience (which might be less dramatic) of how the Holy Spirit helps you?

LET'S PRAY

Oil is often understood as a symbol of the Holy Spirit. You could anoint one another (using olive oil) with the sign of the cross and ask God to fill you with his Holy Spirit.

The spray from this experiment can be violent, so do stand back and make sure your child is a few metres away.

I suggest not showing your child the experiment online first as it will take away some of the thrill.

TOP TIPS

This experiment works best with Diet Coke (the more recently bottled, the better!) because its ingredients are different to other fizzy drinks. The aspartame lowers the surface tension of the liquid much more than corn syrup or sugar.

ADVENTURE 21
Stone Painting

SUMMER

Amateur artists around the world decorate rocks and then hide them in public places. It's often known as pebble painting or rocking. We're going to get arty and then hide our stones. My kids have loved finding some painted stones and we've since created some ourselves.

WHAT YOU DO:

1. The first thing you need to do is find some stones. You can purchase them from a shop or online but I think it's great if the first part of the adventure is finding some. You are looking for pebbles that are small enough to fit in the hand. Ideally they are smooth and have a flatter surface. This is a great summer activity because you can have a day at the beach or by the side of a river, where you can normally find some great stones.

2. After the stones are collected, give them a quick clean in the sink (or if you are really keen leave them to soak in some water for a couple of hours). Then let them dry in a warm place – on the radiator or in the sun (ideally for a day).

3. Put down a tablecloth and get out either some acrylic paint or permanent pens for your design.

4. Before you start, is there a picture or a message that you could put on your stone that would encourage somebody else?

5. Before you decorate, you need to decide whether or not you want to try and track your stone and see where it ends up! If you do, then you will need to join a Facebook group such as 'Love On the Rocks UK' and on the back of your stone write:

   - Post a photo
   - Keep or hide for someone else!

CONTINUED →

6. Get decorating!

7. Finally, to finish your stone, you need to give it a protective coat using either clear nail polish or varnish.

8. Then hide it!

BIBLE TO SHARE
GENESIS 28:10-22 (Bible Overview 1)

Hold a stone and imagine it is your pillow tonight. A man named Jacob, one of God's people in the days before Jesus, once used a stone as a pillow as he prepared for a night under the stars. He had just fled for his life from his own brother and was in an unknown land, alone and exhausted after a fifty-five mile trek. He was completely vulnerable with no protection from the elements, wild animals or other tribes.

It's here, in this place of vulnerability, that he encountered God. He had an incredible vision of a stairway to heaven with angels going up and down. He awoke with these powerful words, 'Surely the Lord is in this place and I didn't even know it.' He renamed this bit of bushland Bethel, which means the House of God. He had fled his father's house, but discovered that his heavenly Father's home is all around.

QUESTIONS TO ASK ...

How would we feel sleeping out under the stars in the wilderness tonight?

How do you think Jacob felt?

What do you think the vision of a stairway to heaven with angels going up and down was like?

If God was present with Jacob, how is he present with us now?

A THOUGHT TO PONDER

'Surely the Lord is in this place, and I was not aware of it.'
What stops us from being aware of God?

LET'S PRAY

Pray that whoever finds your stone will be encouraged
and ask God that he might reveal to them that he is
with them too!

TOP TIPS

Acrylic paints can stain. I'd
recommend wearing aprons.

Small stones and uneven
surfaces are harder to paint.

You might like to do this
activity in two parts –
finding the stones as
one activity and then
the painting and
hiding as another.

AGE RANGE: 3+
EFFORT LEVEL: 4/5
TIMING: 60-120 MINS (DEPENDING
ON HOW MANY STONES YOU MAKE
AND WHERE YOU HIDE THEM)
VITAL EQUIPMENT: STONES
ACRYLIC PAINTS, PAINTBRUSHES
CLEAR NAIL POLISH OR VARNISH, APRON

ADVENTURE 22

Apple Juice Factory

HARVEST

From August until November, the UK has a bountiful harvest of apples to pick. This is your opportunity to venture out beyond the supermarket to collect some apples and make some homemade juice.

WHAT YOU DO:

1. You may have an apple tree in your garden, but the odds are you don't! Living in London, I head with my kids to a nearby apple-picking farm. There are lots of orchards and apple-picking farms around the UK, so find one near you.

2. Get apple picking! You're after sweet apples such as Gala, Rome, Fuji, Honeycrisp or Pink Lady. Here are a few tips on how to pick apples well:

   - Twist the apples rather than pulling them so you don't damage the tree or cause other apples to fall.

   - Hold the apple in the palm of your hand rather than using fingers, so you don't bruise the apple.

   - Only pick ripe apples. They will come away easily from the branch. (You can check by cutting an apple open and seeing if the seeds are brown).

   - Don't drop the apples into your basket. Instead, carefully place them inside so that they don't knock against each other.

   - Wash and then core the apples to remove all the seeds. 16 apples will make about a litre of juice.

3. Cut the apples into slices. You can leave the skin on.

4. Place the slices of apple in a pan and then add water until the pieces of apple are just about covered. Then boil the apples for about 20 to 25 minutes. The apples should become soft.

5. Using a sieve over a large bowl, pour the liquid so that the chunks of apple are caught in the sieve. If you want to keep the juice really fine, then place a coffee filter in the sieve first to catch the sediment.

6. Now gently mash the apples so that the juice will filter through the sieve into the bowl, leaving apple mush.

7. Let the juice cool a bit and then sample it. If it's too strong, add some more water.

8. If you pour the juice into different glasses, you can make some apple juice variations why not add a bit of sugar to one, some honey to another and cinnamon to a third, then give it a stir.

9. Pop the homemade apple juice in the fridge and use it within a week.

BIBLE TO SHARE
LUKE 8:1-15 (Bible Overview 6)

Take some of the apple seeds and ask your child to hold them in their hand, then tell the story from Luke.

Jesus said to his disciples, 'A farmer went out to sow his seed. Some of it fell on the road; it was trampled down and eaten by birds. Other seed fell in the gravel; it sprouted, but it didn't have good roots, so it died. Other seed fell in the weeds; the weeds grew up with it and strangled it. Other seed fell in good soil and produced a great harvest.'

The disciples weren't sure what this meant, so Jesus explained. 'The seed is the Word of God. The seeds on the road are those who hear God's message, but then the devil snatches it away so that they won't be saved. The seeds in the gravel are those who hear eagerly, but it doesn't go very deep. When trouble comes, they quickly forget.

As for the seed that fell in the weeds, these people hear, but then they get distracted by worries or by having a good time, and nothing comes of it. But the seed in the good soil – these are the people who seize the Word and stay with it, holding out until there's a harvest.'

In the parable of the sower, Jesus explains that the harvest is dependent on two factors – the seed and the soil.

CONTINUED →

AGE RANGE: 3+
EFFORT LEVEL: 4/5
TIMING: 60-90 MINS
VITAL EQUIPMENT: APPLES
KITCHEN (WITH PAN AND SIEVE)

QUESTIONS TO ASK ...

Isn't it amazing to think how these seeds become apple trees?

I wonder why Jesus told this story?

Why do you think seeds represent the word of God?

How can we scatter the word of God?

A THOUGHT TO PONDER

There are three different bad soils, but then there's the good soil. A good soil would produce ten times what is sown, and a bumper crop would produce a thirty or forty times increase. But in the good soil that Jesus is talking about, the crop is one hundred times what was sown. This was an abundant harvest! Are our lives this good soil?

LET'S PRAY

Ask God that your lives would be good soil. As you do this, also ask God if there is anything that needs weeding out. If there is, say sorry to God and thank him for his forgiveness.

If you are going to a farm or an orchard, it's worth giving them a call first to check that the apples are ready and to find out the cost.

Be careful with the boiling water.

If you pick more apples, then why not also make some apple crumble?

Don't bin the apple mush! If you puree it and add a touch of sugar and cinnamon, you can make some apple sauce (which you can freeze to use another day).

Some farms and orchards also have pumpkins that you can pick. See the 'Pumpkin Love' adventure (page 76).

ADVENTURE 23

Tabernacles

SEPTEMBER OR OCTOBER

The Israelites had three main pilgrimage festivals each year: Passover (which we now celebrate as Easter), Pentecost, and Sukkot or the Feast of Tabernacles. This is an opportunity to build a camp and explore this ancient festival and what it means for us today as Christians.

WHAT YOU DO:

1. At the Feast of Tabernacles, you need to build a camp. Traditionally, there are four ground rules:
   - Only use one permanent wall to build your camp against.
   - Sparsely cover the roof with branches. You can't use waterproof material and the idea is that you can see the stars.
   - Hang fruit from the roof.
   - Decorate the walls with bright pictures.

2. Now, depending on how adventurous you are, you might like to go full steam ahead and build a tabernacle outside against the back of your home. The frame of a tent will give you a good head start in the construction. If you are feeling really daring and your child is old enough, you might choose to sleep out in sleeping bags and watch the stars.

   Alternatively, you might like to build a camp indoors using items such as cushions, sheets, duvets and clothes racks. Again, you might choose to sleep there overnight or just use it as a day activity.

3. The festival took place when the final harvest was coming in. It was a festival of real joy and so why not create a feast of goodies, perhaps fruit, cake, or chocolate as you explain the significance of the camp that you are now sitting in!

CONTINUED →

BIBLE TO SHARE
LEVITICUS 23:33-36 & 39-43 (Bible Overview 2)

The book of Leviticus was written by Moses and was a series of laws teaching God's people, the Israelites, how to live. Verse 42 explains that the people were to 'live in temporary shelters for seven days'. At different times in Jewish history, this festival has been practiced to differing levels. The Feast of Tabernacles helped God's people remember that they used to be refugees. When they escaped from Egypt they lived in the wilderness for 40 years.

QUESTIONS TO ASK ...

What do you think it would have been like sleeping in a camp like this every night for 40 years?

I wonder why God didn't want the Israelites to forget about this story?

What do you think God might want us to remember as we sit in this camp?

For the Israelites, this feast was one of joy – what can we be joyful about?

A THOUGHT TO PONDER

Jesus goes to Jerusalem during the Feast of Tabernacles in John 7-8. As well as sleeping in outdoor camps, the temple would host various activities. They would set up 16 torches to illuminate the temple courtyard, reminding the people of the glory of God in the wilderness. When Jesus said 'I am the light of the world' in John 8:12, he would have been standing in the light of the torches.

The priests would also do various activities with water, praying for rain in the months ahead. Jesus says in the temple courts, 'If anyone is thirsty, let him come to me and drink' (John 7:37). Jesus was claiming to be more than an ordinary man.

LET'S PRAY

Remember what has given you joy this week.
Say thanks to God.

TOP TIPS

If you are going for the outdoor adventure, then I strongly recommend checking the weather forecast and it's probably best not to do it on a school night!

AGE RANGE: 4+
EFFORT LEVEL: 3/5 - 5/5
TIMING: 40 MINS/ALL NIGHT!
VITAL EQUIPMENT: CAMP BUILDING EQUIPMENT, A FEAST

ADVENTURE 24

Pumpkin Love

31st OCTOBER - HALLOWEEN

Halloween was 'All Hallows' Eve' coming before All Hallows' Day (better known as All Saints' Day, the day we remember men and women of God who have gone before us) and All Souls' Day (remembering those loved ones who have passed). Halloween used to be about celebrating victory over death through Christ – wearing costumes to mock and ridicule the power of death. But today, as parents, it can be difficult to know how much we should engage with this festival. One of the big things my kids want to do is carve a pumpkin!

WHAT YOU DO:

1. The pumpkin has become iconic and stems from the tradition of carving scary faces to either scare others into giving some kind of gift or to scare away evil spirits. As Christians, we believe that God's love demonstrated in the cross of Jesus is the ultimate power, and so we're going to carve either a heart or a cross. It might be helpful to explain this to your child before you begin.

2. Get the right pumpkin – ideally one that's fresh. You are looking for a pumpkin with a firm stem and ideally no bruises. A flat bottom will also stop it from rolling away!

3. Using something like a boning knife, I recommend you cut a circle in the bottom of the pumpkin, not the top. This will stop the lid from falling in!

4. Once your hole is created, start scooping the pulp out. An ice cream scoop can prove handy and this is the kind of task your child can get stuck into! The idea is to leave the wall of the pumpkin about 5cm thick so that it's not too deep to carve into.

5. Get your child to draw the heart or cross shape on paper first. They might like to do both – one on either side of the pumpkin. Once the design is ready, cut it out and then, holding it against the pumpkin, use a knife to poke holes along the outline. As you carve out your design, clean lines look best, so get those edges looking sharp.

6. If you want to keep your pumpkin looking fresh, you can rub some Vaseline into the outside skin which will help lock in the moisture.

7. Put either a wax candle or a battery-operated candle in the pumpkin.

8. Why not use the pulp to make some pumpkin soup or pumpkin pie?

BIBLE TO SHARE

DANIEL 6 (Bible Overview 5)

With the candle alight, tell the story of Daniel and the Lions' Den. As you tell the story, ask your child to imagine that they are Daniel.

In the days before Jesus came to earth, God's people, the Israelites, were captured once again and taken to a place called Babylon. A man named Daniel, who loved God and obeyed him, became an advisor to the king of Babylon, but the other advisors plotted against him. They got the king to make a new law that said, 'No-one can pray to anyone except the king!' Now, this was a problem for Daniel, because he prayed to God three times a day. But he still chose to carry on praying to God, and because of this he was arrested and thrown into a den of lions. But God shut the mouths of the lions, so that Daniel would not be hurt, and he was released from the den in the morning – without a scratch on him!

QUESTIONS TO ASK ...

What animal do you think is the scariest?

What do you think the lions looked like?

How would you have felt if you were Daniel left alone for a night with lions?

Do you think God always protects his people?

Is there anything you are scared of today?

CONTINUED →

AGE RANGE: 4+
EFFORT LEVEL: 4/5
TIMING: 60 MINS
VITAL EQUIPMENT: A PUMPKIN, CARVING UTENSILS, TEA-LIGHT CANDLE, AND MATCHES

A THOUGHT TO PONDER

Being a follower of Jesus doesn't guarantee that we will always be saved from the difficult things that happen in our lives, but we find this beautiful promise in Romans 8:38-39:

'For I am convinced that neither death nor life, neither angels nor demons, neither the present nor the future, nor any powers, neither height nor depth, nor anything else in all creation, will be able to separate us from the love of God that is in Christ Jesus our Lord.'

Thinking on this verse, what might God speak into our fears this Halloween?

LET'S PRAY

Look at the symbol of the cross and/or the heart on the pumpkin and as you do, bring any fears to God and ask him for a deeper understanding of his love.

Sharp knives can be dangerous. Be really careful when carving your pumpkin.

Don't leave a lit candle unattended!

ADVENTURE 25
Leaf Art

AUTUMN

In the autumn the ground is laden with twigs, conkers and a multitude of coloured leaves. This adventure is about creating a masterpiece together using the autumnal debris.

WHAT YOU DO:

1. Find a location where there are lots of leaves on the floor, ideally with a rich variety of colours.

2. Go rummaging and collect whatever you can find. Hopefully, there will be lots of leaves. Create piles of different coloured leaves.

3. Once you have a good bounty of material, decide on what image you want to create. Could it be a monster? Or a family portrait?

4. Map out your frame. You might like to use a piece of tarp on the ground for this as it will give you a background colour. Depending on how much you have collected, your masterpiece could be the size of your hands, or as big as a person.

5. As you get designing, it's usually best to create the base images first and to leave the detail for the very end.

6. Take a picture of your work of art. If you take a stepladder or selfie stick, you can get a good shot from above. You might even like to have your child in the picture. (Perhaps they are being eaten by the monster!)

CONTINUED →

BIBLE TO SHARE

ISAIAH 40:8 (Bible Overview 4)

Isaiah was a prophet in the Old Testament, before Jesus came. A prophet is someone who shares messages from God's heart. In his book, he shares about the tough times that lie ahead for the people of Israel but in chapter 40 he comforts God's people. Isaiah 40:8 reads, 'The grass withers and the flowers fall, but the word of our God endures forever.'

QUESTIONS TO ASK ...

What's your favourite season?

How will this place change as the seasons change?

What kind of changes lie ahead in our lives?

What are some of the promises of God that are unchanging, that we can hold on to, even when we go through changing seasons?

Here are some suggestions to get you started:

'Come near to God and he will come near to you' (James 4:8).

'Ask and it will be given to you; seek and you will find; knock and the door will be opened to you' (Matthew 7:7).

'Jesus said to her, "I am the resurrection and the life. The one who believes in me will live, even though they die"' (John 11:25-26).

'If you declare with your mouth, "Jesus is Lord," and believe in your heart that God raised him from the dead, you will be saved' (Romans 10:9).

A THOUGHT TO PONDER

In the New Testament, Peter refers to this passage explaining that as Christians, the enduring word that Isaiah spoke about is the Gospel message – the message of Jesus (1 Peter 1:23-25). How does that truth impact how we live in an ever-changing world? You might like to share how much the world has changed since you were a child, and a simple truth about God that has remained the same throughout your life.

LET'S PRAY

Gather all the leaves together in a massive pile and then throw them in the air. As you do this, thank God that his word will not die like these leaves.

AGE RANGE: 3+
EFFORT LEVEL: 3/5
TIMING: 30-60 MINS
VITAL EQUIPMENT:
TARPAULIN (OPTIONAL)
STEPLADDER (OPTIONAL)
SELFIE STICK (OPTIONAL)

TOP TIPS

If you choose to use a stepladder, be careful!

ADVENTURE 26

Generous Advent(ure)

WINTER

At Christmas time, most kids are looking forward to the presents that they might receive. They might write a list for Santa or leave subtle hints about what they'd like to receive. With this as the backdrop, it's really good to encourage our children about how we can serve others and live generously. This adventure is about trying to bless as many people as possible without getting any credit!

WHAT YOU DO:

1. Think through who you can bless in your community. With your child think through what you could do and try not to get any credit for it. The idea is that this is a stealth adventure where people are blessed but have no idea who did it!

2. Here are a few ideas to get you thinking …

   You could:
   - Take a bin liner and go and clean up some rubbish from the park
   - Spruce up somewhere with some Christmas decorations
   - Write a thank you card and deliver it to the local police station
   - Bake cakes for someone in your community who might appreciate them
   - Buy a homeless person a coffee or lunch
   - Draw a picture to encourage the fire brigade at your local station
   - Put out a box of chocolates with a note for the bin crew
   - Buy some goodies for the food bank to give away
   - Clean the rest of the family's bikes
   - Go and clean something in the church building
   - Buy someone flowers and leave them on their doorstep with an encouraging note

BIBLE TO SHARE
MATTHEW 1:18-24 (Bible Overview 6)

A young woman called Mary, who lived in Israel, was visited by an angel who told her that she would give birth to the son of God, Jesus. Joseph, the man who was going to marry her, had a dream in which the angel said to him that Jesus would be called Immanuel, which means 'God with us.'

QUESTIONS TO ASK ...

What is the most generous or kindest thing someone has done for you?

How have you been generous or kind to someone else?

How do you think God is generous or kind to us? What does Christmas show us about this?

How might knowing this about God impact how we live our lives?

A THOUGHT TO PONDER

Holding my daughter's first pink stripy Babygro is a powerful reminder of how small she once was. It's mind-blowing to think how much she has grown, and more so to think that I once used to fill one of these tiny outfits myself. Even more astonishing is that God entered humanity as a baby. He came to be with us. Not born into a palace, but into obscurity.

LET'S PRAY

Thank God for his kindness and generosity and then pray very simply the following phrase several times:

'God, make us aware that you are with us.'

Then spend one minute just being quiet and see if you feel God in some way.

What makes this challenge exciting is trying not to get caught blessing other people. However, if you do get caught in the act of generosity, don't worry about it too much, just explain what you are doing.

TOP TIPS

AGE RANGE: **3+**
EFFORT LEVEL: **VARIOUS**
TIMING: **VARIOUS**
VITAL EQUIPMENT: **VARIOUS**

Adventure stories are normally about thin...
shipwrecked boats and marooned sailor...
mountains and intrepid mountaineers. B...
somewhere physically, but about goi...
It's about an attitude. This selecti...
home, but with our imaginatio...
the size of a h...

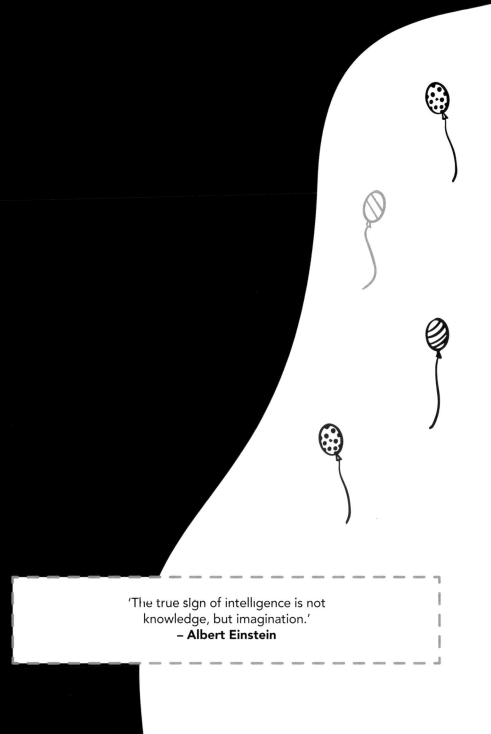

'The true sign of intelligence is not knowledge, but imagination.'
– Albert Einstein

ADVENTURE 27

Lemonade Making

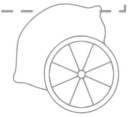

We often turn on the taps and don't think about where our water comes from. This mini adventure is an opportunity to collect your own water and make some lemonade!

WHAT YOU DO:

1. For this adventure you're going to need rain. So check out the forecast the week ahead.

2. Find a flat piece of grass and set out the tarpaulin on the floor. The ground needs to be soft enough that you can push sticks into it (this will be difficult if the ground is really hard).

3. Take the first of the four sticks and then go to the first corner of the tarp. Push the stick into the ground at a slight angle so that it is looking away from the centre of the tarpaulin. Then using the string, tie the top of the stick to the tarp.

4. Repeat this for all four corners so that the tarp is completely off the ground. At the same time, make sure the tarp is not taut but that it has some sag.

5. Go to the very centre of the plastic sheet and make a hole with a biro or a skewer. Underneath the hole, position your bowl. Now as the rain falls, the water will collect in your bowl.

6. Once you have collected some water (the quantity will obviously depend on how heavy the rainfall is and the size of the plastic sheet), ask your child to sample it. Does it taste different to water from the tap?

7. To make lemonade, chop up three lemons (the flesh, not the rind) and add them to 140g of caster sugar and half a litre of the water that you have collected. Then pour the mixture into a blender and turn it on until the lemon is finely chopped.

8. Then pour the mixture out into a bowl, using a sieve to filter out the sediment. It might be helpful to use a spoon to press through as much of the juice as you can. Finally, top up the mixture with another half litre of water.

BIBLE TO SHARE

JOHN 2:1-11 (Bible Overview 6)

Tell your child the story of Jesus turning the water into wine. If they have been to a wedding before, maybe ask them to reflect on what it was like.

The first miracle that Jesus did was at a wedding he went to with his disciples and his mother. At the party after the ceremony, Jesus' mother Mary saw that they had nearly run out of wine. She told Jesus, but he said to her, 'We don't need to get involved, Mother. It isn't my time just yet.' But Mary went ahead anyway, telling the servants, 'Do whatever he tells you.' There were six huge stone pots there, which the servants filled with water as Jesus instructed them. Then Jesus told them to draw some out and take it to the host. When the host tasted it, he said to the bridegroom, 'Everyone else starts with the finest wine and then later brings out the cheap stuff. But you have saved the best until last!'

You might like to share that at the time, a wedding could last for over a week! The bridegroom had to provide food and drink for all the guests during that period and if he failed to do so it would have brought disgrace on his family.

QUESTIONS TO ASK ...

Do you think Jesus liked weddings?

How would you have felt if you were the bridegroom and all the wine had run out?

What might have happened if Mary hadn't spoken to Jesus?

I wonder why Jesus did this miracle?

What does this story show us about Jesus?

AGE RANGE: 3+
EFFORT LEVEL: 4/5
TIMING: 60 MINS (WITH EXTRA TIME FOR THE WATER TO COLLECT)
VITAL EQUIPMENT: PLASTIC SHEET OR TARP, STRING, FOUR STICKS, BOWL, 140G CASTER SUGAR, BLENDER, SIEVE, 3 LEMONS

A THOUGHT TO PONDER

Jesus asks the servants to do something quite strange – to fill up six stone jars with water, and then take some of that to the host. Why do you think they obeyed him?

In John 2:11, it says that the disciples believed in Jesus because of this miracle. Why is that, do you think?

In what ways does God ask us to do some strange things, and how might he use our obedience to do something incredible?

LET'S PRAY

Jesus, help us remember this story when we are facing difficult situations.
Help us to be like Mary, coming to you.
Help us to be like the servants, obeying you.
Help us to be like the disciples, believing in you.
Amen.

TOP TIPS

If you don't collect enough water to make the lemonade, then you could use the water that you have collected to make ice cubes for the lemonade.

ADVENTURE 28

Bugs!

There are all kinds of bugs around us, especially in our gardens. This little adventure is about seeing what kind of bugs are in our area by building an insect trap!

WHAT YOU DO:

1. Find somewhere outside that is rarely disturbed. For example, a flower bed at the back of the garden or in a nearby park.

2. Get some containers – such as jam jars or yogurt pots.

3. Put some pieces of fruit in the containers, such as some slices of banana.

4. Take your containers to the quiet spot in the garden or park. Dig a little hole in the ground and place your containers in the hole. The containers should only be buried up to the rim.

5. Next, take some stones and place them around the edge of the container. Rest a larger rock on top of the stones, so that the container is fully hidden. The stones act as a support for the bigger rock and protect the containers from rain whilst also creating a small gap for the insects to crawl under and into the pot.

6. Leave the traps at least a couple of hours but ideally overnight.

7. Remove the rock and see what you have caught! If you have a magnifying glass, you might like to encourage your child to inspect what they have and see if they can determine what kind of insect it is.

8. Finally, release the insects once you have finished analysing them!

CONTINUED →

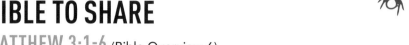

BIBLE TO SHARE
MATTHEW 3:1-6 (Bible Overview 6)

There are some fascinating people in the Bible. These few verses tell us about John the Baptist, who wore a cloak of camel's hair (not comfortable!) and ate wild honey and insects called locusts. Locusts are a bit like a large grasshopper, and still eaten by people in some countries, including Kuwait and Mexico. In some places, locusts are eaten covered in chocolate! Do you think you would enjoy a chocolate-covered locust? Maybe John ate his locusts dipped in the honey!

John was probably around thirty years old, and lived in the wilderness by the River Jordan. Just before Jesus started to preach the good news about God's rescue plan, John started to tell people, 'God's Kingdom is near. Repent and change your ways!' Many people came from all around to hear him, and for those who wanted to change their lives, John baptised them in the River Jordan.

QUESTIONS TO ASK ...

How do you think John caught the locusts he ate? Do you reckon they were tasty?

Why do you think many people went out to see him?

Would you have gone out to see him?

John's message to the people was to 'repent' which means to change direction. In what ways do you think God asks us to change in our lives today?

A THOUGHT TO PONDER

Both Isaiah and Malachi (two of God's prophets) had spoken about the coming of John hundreds of years before his birth. This was part of God's plan. John's job was to point the people towards Jesus.

You might like to show your child the painting by Annibale Carracci called 'Saint John the Baptist in a landscape pointing at the figure of Christ.' What do they think about this painting?

How do we point to Jesus with our lives today?

LET'S PRAY

In John 3:30, John the Baptist says these words about Jesus: 'He must increase, but I must decrease.' (ESV)

Perhaps with a recognition of how God might be asking us to change, we can ask God to help us do that so that we can point to Jesus more effectively.

The website www.insectidentification.org has a bug finder tool to help you work out exactly what you have caught. Alternatively, there are some insect identification apps available on iPhone and Android, such as Picture Insect.

TOP TIPS

AGE RANGE: 3+
EFFORT LEVEL: 2/5
TIMING: 30 MINS (THEN IDEALLY OVERNIGHT)
VITAL EQUIPMENT: CONTAINERS (SUCH AS JAM JARS OR YOGURT POTS) STONES, FRUIT, MAGNIFYING GLASS (OPTIONAL)

ADVENTURE 29

Prayer Scroll

We're going to create an ancient prayer scroll that can help us pray the Lord's Prayer over the next week.

WHAT YOU DO:

1. You need a piece of A4 paper with the Lord's Prayer on it. Ideally the paper would be white and good quality. You might choose to print it as a Word document (allowing your child to choose which font looks really old in style!). Or if your child can write, then they can copy the words out. If they are younger, you can pencil the words for them to write over, and if they are older, you could look at some calligraphy fonts and see how creative they can be.

2. To make the prayer scroll look old, crumple the paper into a ball several times.

3. Take a used damp teabag and wipe it over both sides of the paper to turn the prayer scroll a light brown colour. You will need to leave it to dry after this.

4. Then work on the edges. You can either carefully tear all the edges off the four sides of the paper to make the prayer scroll look tattered. Or if your child is a bit older, you can carefully burn the edges of the prayer scroll. If you are going to do this then be cautious, doing it over a baking tray and ideally outside so that the fire alarm is not set off.

5. Finally, give your prayer scroll a wax seal. To do this, light a tea light (ideally a colourful one – I used red) and let the wax drip into a little puddle on the scroll. Then, as it cools and begins to solidify, make a thumb print in the wax. Then let the wax dry fully.

BIBLE TO SHARE

MATTHEW 6:9-13 (Bible Overview 6)

Jesus taught the disciples how to pray, and this prayer is now said in countries around the globe in hundreds of languages every single day. As you read through each couple of lines from your prayer scroll, ask your child what they think this means.

QUESTIONS TO ASK ...

What do you think prayer is?

What do you like best about this prayer?

Is it good to have written prayers like this?

Why do you think Jesus taught us to pray this prayer?

A THOUGHT TO PONDER

In Luke 11:1, we discover that the disciples ask Jesus how to pray. There was something about how Jesus prayed that was unique and special. He gives us this template. What happens when we pray this prayer regularly, reflecting on the words?

LET'S PRAY

Why not see if you can pray this prayer every day for a week? You could stick the prayer scroll to the wall to pray each night before bed or find different places to pray this prayer. For example, is there a high building you could go to the top of to pray this prayer, or a church crypt that would give a nice echo?

TOP TIPS

When burning paper and making the wax seal, use real caution. If you do go for burning the edges of the scroll, it's best to do a little bit at a time rather than risk destroying your child's masterpiece!

AGE RANGE: 4+
EFFORT LEVEL: 3/5
TIMING: 40 MINS
VITAL EQUIPMENT: PAPER PEN OR PRINTER, COLOURFUL TEA LIGHT, TEABAG, MATCHES

ADVENTURE 30

Adventure in Bubbles

Making bubbles is always entertaining, but when you get to make your own bubbles and create some huge ones, it can really amp up the fun factor for both you and your kids!

WHAT YOU DO:

1. First of all, you're going to make your bubble mixture. To do so, you will need a washing-up bowl (or a mixing bowl) and the ingredients: water, washing-up liquid and glycerine (which can be found in the baking section of the supermarket). When it comes to choosing the ingredients for your bubble liquid, the better quality stuff is generally more effective for making bubbles.

2. For every 300ml water, you will need 50ml washing-up liquid and a tablespoon of glycerine. This will make a good amount of mixture but if you want to make more, then you can use these ratios.

3. Start with the washing-up liquid. The back of the bottle will give you a quantity and the mixture normally comes in 500ml containers. You might find it helpful to use a mixing jug with ml markings on the side to measure out 50ml washing-up liquid, and then add it to your bowl.

4. Then carefully add the water. You want to try not to create bubbles as you're pouring the water into the container. Then add the glycerine (which makes the mixture more stable).

5. Very gently, stir the mixture with a spoon or even a chopstick, again trying not to create any bubbles. If you do create bubbles, remove the foam as it is created.

6. Ideally you would then let the bubble mixture rest so that it can settle. If you can wait overnight, the bubbles will be even better!

7. Now here's the challenge – what can you find around the house to make bubbles with? Here are a few ideas: paperclips, floral wire, kitchen towel tubing, pipe cleaners, wire hangers or a colander! This could become a bit of a creative scavenger hunt!

8. Then you can show your child how to make giant bubble sticks! To do so, you need two sticks and two pieces of string. One piece of string needs to be 1m long and the other 80cm long. Tie the 80cm long string to one end of both of the sticks. Then tie the longer piece of string to either end of the shorter piece of string (and not the stick!) When you now lift it up and pull the sticks apart, the shorter string should be taut, and the longer string should have slack and hang down, making an arch. When you soak the string in the bubble mixture and then gently pull the sticks apart you'll create massive bubbles!

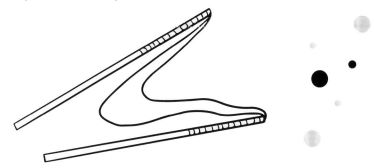

BIBLE TO SHARE

GENESIS 9:8-17 (Bible Overview 1)

We often focus on the story of Noah and the animals, but it's good to reflect on what happened after the flood. You might like to ask your child if they can tell you the story of Noah before you look at these verses.

This passage talks about God's covenant, which is God's promise and agreed relationship with his people. Note that this agreement isn't just with the people but the entirety of creation!

After the floodwaters went down and Noah and his family left the Ark, God said to Noah, 'I'm making a covenant with you and all who come after you, that I will never again send a flood on the earth. When you see a rainbow appear in the sky, this will be a sign; I will remember the covenant promise that I made to you and to all living things on the earth.'

CONTINUED →

QUESTIONS TO ASK ...

When you were making your bubbles, did you see any rainbows?

Why do you think God makes promises to people?

What do you do when someone makes a promise to you?

A THOUGHT TO PONDER

The word for rainbow in Hebrew is keshet, also meaning 'war bow.' In a sense, God is hanging up his bow. The rainbow is a sign of God's promise to humankind, but the cross is the ultimate sign of God's promise to us.

LET'S PRAY

What promises do you think God has made to you?
Thank him for them.

TOP TIPS

This is definitely an outdoor activity and weather will impact bubble capacity. Warmer days work best and if there is wind, you can use it to your advantage.

Be careful when using wire and hangers as they can be sharp.

AGE RANGE: 3+
EFFORT LEVEL: 3/5
TIMING: 45 MINS (WITH IDEALLY AN OVERNIGHT FOR THE LIQUID TO SETTLE)
VITAL EQUIPMENT: WATER, WASHING-UP LIQUID, WASHING-UP BOWL, GLYCERINE TWO STICKS, STRING AND SCISSORS

ADVENTURE
31
Rocket Man

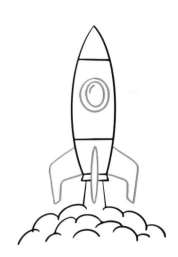

This little adventure is all about building a rocket! Fuelled by vinegar and baking soda, there are a variety of ways to build both your rocket and the launch pad. This one is (for me) the simplest and if you nail it, you can get some serious height!

WHAT YOU DO:

1. The first thing you need to do is build your rocket from an empty two-litre plastic bottle. The bottom of the bottle will actually be the top of the rocket, and the top of the bottle will be the bottom of the rocket. So that the bottle can stand upside down, you will need to add three legs. You can do this by taking three (ideally blunt) pencils or wooden sticks and taping them with gaffer tape to the bottle. The three legs need to be level so as to keep the top of the bottle off the ground. Once this is done, your bottle should now be able to stand on its new legs.

2. You can then add further decorations, but be aware that the heavier the bottle, the less height it is likely to get and the decorations may well come off! You could simply use permanent markers to draw pictures or stripes on the rocket.

3. Find a cork for the bottle and check it goes in OK.

4. Put the rocket on its head (on the bottom of the bottle) and fill it half full with vinegar.

5. Take three tablespoons of baking soda and put them onto the centre of one piece of kitchen paper. Then roll the kitchen paper up with the baking soda inside tightly, a bit like you are making a fajita. The baking soda should not be able to fall out, but you must also make sure that it will still be able to fit through the bottle neck.

CONTINUED →

6. Head outside. Now remember, you can get some serious height with this rocket, so you need to be away from main roads, electricity pylons etc.

7. I strongly suggest you wear eye goggles for this part! Carefully lower the baking soda packet through the neck of the bottle and use the cork to fix it in place. The cork should be on firmly but not too tight. The parcel of baking soda should now be hanging a few centimetres away from the vinegar inside the bottle.

8. Finally tip the bottle upside down so that the rocket is standing on its three legs. Move away quickly and safely as now the vinegar and the baking soda will start reacting. As they react they will force the cork off and ... woosh! Up goes the rocket!

9. You can then repeat this to your heart's content! It might be that you set the rocket off the first time but if your child feels comfortable, then maybe they would like to try it the second time.

BIBLE TO SHARE

ACTS 1:6-11 (Bible Overview 7)

After Jesus had risen from the dead, he spent forty days with his disciples talking about his Kingdom. The disciples wanted to know the specifics of what God's plan was, but Jesus told them, 'Don't worry about the timing of it all. My Father has that all in hand. But you will receive power to tell people everywhere about me, even to the ends of the earth, when the Holy Spirit comes upon you.' After this, Jesus was lifted up to heaven on a cloud, and as they stood watching he faded from their sight. When they looked around, they saw two angels in white nearby. 'Why are you standing and staring, men of Galilee?' the angels asked. 'Jesus has been taken up into heaven now, and when he comes back he will arrive in just this same way.'

QUESTIONS TO ASK ...

How do you think Jesus ascended into heaven? Do you think it was like the rocket?

Do you think the disciples missed Jesus after he ascended?

Why do you think the disciples kept looking up at the clouds after Jesus had left?

How do you think it will be when one day Jesus returns?

A THOUGHT TO PONDER

Jesus is no longer here in physical form, but he sent his Holy Spirit at Pentecost to equip the disciples to be like Jesus. In many ways, we are called to be the hands and feet of Jesus. What might this look like?

LET'S PRAY

We can pray in different positions. Why not pray with your hands open on your lap, as if you were playing pass the parcel. Our posture shows God that we are expectantly looking to receive his Holy Spirit.

Spend a moment asking God for his Holy Spirit to help us be like Jesus.

This must be done outside!

Stand at least 2 metres away from the rocket and be aware that it may take 10 to 15 seconds for the rocket to take off. If the rocket fails to take off, then you may have secured the cork too tightly – in which case taking off the cork can be a very messy experience.

TOP TIPS

I strongly suggest wearing something over your eyes, as vinegar in the eyes is not comfortable!

Before I did this for the first time, I watched several videos online so I knew what to expect. However I would recommend not showing your child beforehand so that they can really enjoy the moment.

AGE RANGE: 8+
EFFORT LEVEL: 4/5
TIMING: 40 MINS
VITAL EQUIPMENT: EMPTY PLASTIC BOTTLE, VINEGAR, BAKING SODA, CORK WOODEN STICKS OR PENCILS (FOR LAUNCHING PAD), GAFFER TAPE (OTHER TAPES ALSO WORK)

ADVENTURE 32

Egg Drop

This adventure is an opportunity to create an egg man and then send him on a great adventure from a first floor window with a child-made parachute.

WHAT YOU DO:

1. Show your child the egg. You might like to give it a name and draw some eyes and a mouth on with a marker pen. Explain that the egg is soon about to have the biggest adventure ever, being dropped out of a first floor window. The challenge is to build a parachute for the egg, so that it will survive when it is dropped.

2. Give your child a variety of items to construct their parachute with. For example: pipe cleaners, a plastic bag, some Blu-Tack, some sellotape, string, a sheet of paper, some kitchen roll, paperclips, a small cardboard box, scissors.

3. Before they get making, they might like to think through and even talk through the design. Depending on the age of the child, you might want to make it with them or, if they are older, have a competition to see which of you can make the best egg parachute, maybe within a fixed time limit of say 30 minutes.

4. When the parachute is constructed, head up to the first floor window. When it comes to leaning out of windows, I would suggest that you do this and that your child goes and stands by the drop zone.

5. Drop the egg, making sure that it does not hit the side of the wall or anyone below as it falls down.

6. Finally, inspect the egg. Did it make it?

TOP TIPS

If your egg survives the first floor drop, you may choose to go higher!

Do be careful with leaning out of windows and make sure there is no-one underneath.

BIBLE TO SHARE

MATTHEW 14:22-33 (Bible Overview 6)

This is the classic story of Peter walking on water. Just beforehand, Jesus had fed the 5,000 and dismissed the huge crowd.

After the crowd had gone home, Jesus went up a mountain by himself to pray, telling his disciples to get into their boat and go to the other side of the lake. As darkness fell, a stormy wind was whipping up the waves of the lake, and at about four o'clock in the morning the disciples saw Jesus walking towards them on top of the waves. They were terrified, saying, 'It's a ghost!' But Jesus called to them, 'Be brave! It's me.' Peter said, 'Lord, if it's really you, then tell me to come to you on the waves.' Jesus said, 'Come on, then.'

So Peter climbed out of the boat and started walking on the waves towards Jesus. But as soon as he took his eyes off Jesus and focused on the storm around him, he panicked and started to sink. 'Lord, save me!' he cried. Jesus immediately stretched out his hand to take Peter's and pull him to safety. 'Ah, Peter, what little faith you have! Why did you doubt?' he said. When they got into the boat, the storm immediately subsided, and the other disciples were amazed, saying to Jesus, 'We can see that you really are the Son of God!'

QUESTIONS TO ASK ...

If you were the egg, would you have trusted the parachute that you had made?

What do you think it would be like to parachute out of a plane? Would you ever want to do it?

What do you think it was like for Peter to climb out of the boat and walk to Jesus on the water?

I wonder why Peter trusted Jesus when he called him out of the boat?

A THOUGHT TO PONDER

Peter was able to walk on the water when he was looking at Jesus. But as soon as his focus shifted from Jesus to the wind, he began to sink. What lessons can we learn from this for our lives?

LET'S PRAY

Think about some of the different situations you will find yourself in during the week ahead. Pray that you would keep your focus not on the wind, but on Jesus.

AGE RANGE: 3+
EFFORT LEVEL: 3/5
TIMING: 40 MINS
VITAL EQUIPMENT:
EGGS, VARIOUS CRAFT MATERIALS

ADVENTURE 33

Slime Factory

My kids love slime. There are many ways of creating it. Here are two simple recipes to start with (see ingredients overleaf). Each ingredient is important in creating the perfect mixture.

WHAT YOU DO:

Basic Slime

1. Get yourself a bowl and pour in about 200 grams of PVA glue. Then add a teaspoon of bicarbonate of soda and get mixing!

2. Add some gel food colouring into the mixture and stir it in thoroughly so that it is totally integrated.

3. Now add one tablespoon of contact lens solution. This is a fine art! If the slime remains really sticky, you may need to add a touch more solution but if there is too much, then the slime can become hard and break.

4. Mix the solution in with a spoon. It should start to become stringy and when it does, move it onto the kitchen surface to knead it with your hands.

5. After a minute of kneading, you now have slime. If you want to make it extra fun, you can add some glitter.

6. You can also now try repeating the process with different food colourings to make various colours of slime.

Fluffy Slime

1. Get yourself a bowl and pour in about 200 grams of PVA glue. Then add the food colouring to get the colour you want.

2. Add shaving cream (approximately three times the amount of the glue) and mix well.

3. As the mixture gets thick and fluffy, it's time to add the contact lens solution. Add a few drops at a time, stirring thoroughly until you get the right slime consistency.

BIBLE TO SHARE
GENESIS 1:24-25 (Bible Overview 1)

As you feel the slime between your fingers, read the story of God creating animals from Genesis. As you read these words, ask your child to try and picture what is happening.

God spoke, saying, 'Let there be all kinds of living creatures on the earth' – and it happened! All sorts of animals – cows and sheep, lizards and bugs, bears, lions, elephants and more – were created. Every animal was created by God.

QUESTIONS TO ASK ...

How was it creating the slime?

What else have you created so far in life? What is the best thing about creating things?

How do you think God felt when he was creating the world?

God describes everything he makes as good. What are your favourite things in creation?

A THOUGHT TO PONDER

Creation is not made static and finished, but everything is laden with potential. In the next chapter of Genesis (2:15), God commands humans to work with and take care of creation. This can be translated as 'to serve and preserve creation.' God gives humans the role of looking after his creation. What does that mean?

CONTINUED →

LET'S PRAY

Say this prayer together:

This world,
Your creation,
Rolled into a sphere,
Packaged in sunshine,
Gift-wrapped in love,
Given to us,
Thank you.

(courtesy of faithandworship.com)

The glue must be a PVA-based glue. (It's the type used in schools.)

The slime can stick to fabric, so best to wear an apron!

You can store basic slime in an airtight container,
but fluffy slime will lose its fluffiness.

It's always good to wash hands before
and after playing with slim

TOP TIPS

AGE RANGE: 3+
EFFORT LEVEL: 3/5
TIMING: 15 MINS
VITAL EQUIPMENT: SEE BELOW

BASIC SLIME:
200 GRAMS OF PVA OR CLEAR GLUE
BICARBONATE OF SODA
CONTACT LENS SOLUTION (NOTE: IT MUST CONTAIN BORIC ACID/BORAX)
GEL FOOD COLOURING

FLUFFY SLIME:
200 GRAMS OF PVA OR CLEAR GLUE
SHAVING CREAM
CONTACT LENS SOLUTION (NOTE: IT MUST CONTAIN BORIC ACID/BORAX)
GEL FOOD COLOURING

ADVENTURE 34

Cardboard Fort

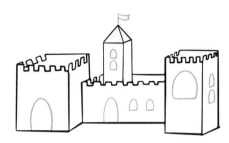

Give a child a cardboard box and they will have hours of fun! This adventure is about building a cardboard fort. It's an opportunity to go big and work with your child in construction, whilst exploring the story of Esther.

WHAT YOU DO:

1. First of all you need some cardboard! You can buy it online but we normally build forts after we've had something delivered or by going to the supermarket and asking for some old cardboard boxes. Make sure they are dry. If the boxes have already been flattened, then you can reassemble them with some tape. The more boxes you can get, the bigger the fort you can build!

2. Start with the biggest box you have, with the open end facing up, and have some parcel tape on hand to connect the next box. To make the adjoining boxes more secure, it's often best to align the next box with the edge of the main box, creating a flat surface. This will make sticking them together easier.

3. Once the second box is in place, carefully cut out a doorway or tunnel to make a route through. If you are cutting sections out, keep the excess cardboard as it could be helpful for making some features once the main fort is built.

4. As you build, here are some ideas to take your fort to the next level:

   - Cut a door as an entrance, or if you are feeling really creative and have some string to hand, you could make a drawbridge!

   - Add a roof, either by cutting and sticking excess cardboard together or by simply throwing a sheet over the top.

   - Keep expanding, adjoining multiple boxes, and maybe making a tunnel that leads to another part of the fort.

105

CONTINUED →

- Add windows by cutting out shapes in the side. These will also help let light in.

- If it's dark inside, then is there a torch that your child could borrow or even some Christmas tree lights that you could use?

- Encourage your child to make it comfortable inside. Why not bring a duvet and some pillows inside?

- Finally, does your fort need some decoration? Whether you want to get the paints out or stick some old wallpaper on the sides, think about how you can give it the extra wow factor.

BIBLE TO SHARE
ESTHER 5:1-3 (Bible Overview 5)

Queen Esther was the wife of the King of Persia, and she was a Jew (one of God's people). When the Jewish people in Persia were under threat, she had the opportunity to save her people by asking to see the king. Even though she was the queen, she was not allowed to approach the throne without permission. Unless the king's sceptre was extended towards her, she would be put to death. She bravely chose to go before the king with a plan to save her people. As she approached, the gold sceptre was lowered towards her, allowing her to talk with the king.

Why not read these verses inside the fort?

QUESTIONS TO ASK ...

What do you think it would have been like to live in a castle?

In the story of Esther, she risks her life to try and save her people. What risky things might we do because they are the right thing to do?

In the book of Esther, God isn't mentioned at all but he is at work continuously behind the scenes. How might God be at work even when we haven't recognised him?

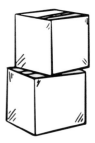

A THOUGHT TO PONDER

The King of kings has lowered his gold sceptre to us by giving his son Jesus to us. The life, death, and resurrection of Jesus means that we can come to God without fear and with any request we have.

LET'S PRAY

Take a chair and pretend it's a throne. Imagine that God is sitting on the throne. Kneel down in front of the chair and bring any requests you have to God.

TOP TIPS

If you want to take fort-building to another level, then you can buy sheets of corrugated cardboard. There are then a variety of templates online that you can use to make a much more robust fortress.

Get your child as involved as you can but if you are using sharp scissors or a Stanley knife, then be really careful and keep them out of your child's reach when you're not using them.

AGE RANGE: 3+
EFFORT LEVEL: 4/5
TIMING: 90-120 MINS
VITAL EQUIPMENT: CARDBOARD, TAPE
SHARP SCISSORS OR STANLEY KNIFE

ADVENTURE 35

Adventure in Music

I'm not very musical, but my kids both love making instruments and creating noise. I think it's important to encourage them in music, whether we are musical or not. This mini adventure is all about creating instruments and then exploring Psalm 100.

WHAT YOU DO:

You could create any or all of these:

1. **Drums** – At the most basic level, you can get some pots and pans out of the kitchen and give your child a wooden spoon or some chopsticks. Try and teach them to keep a beat!

    If you want to take it a step further, then find some tubs and tubes and make a drum skin using brown packing tape by laying it across the end. Different size containers will make different sounds.

2. **Rainstick** – Make a rainstick using a cardboard tube. Seal it at one end, add some beans and then seal it at the other end. Teach your child to tip it slowly from end to end, listening to the soothing sounds. You can add some decoration using ribbons or coloured paper.

3. **Egg Shakers** – Place some beads or rice in small containers (such as Kinder Egg boxes or plastic kitchen storage boxes). Then get shaking!

4. **Classic Guitar** – Take a cereal box and make a hole in the middle. Then fix five elastic bands around the box and so that they cross the centre of the hole. Different elastic bands will make different sounds. (You can also build a neck for your guitar using the centre of a kitchen roll.)

5. **Bottle Melodies** – Take a selection of bottles and fill them up with differing amounts of water (don't fill them to the top). Now rest your bottom lip on the top and blow gently across the top until you can hear a note. Check out how different sizes of bottles and amounts of water change the sound.

BIBLE TO SHARE

PSALM 100 (Bible Overview 3)

Read through this psalm once, and then ask your child what sounds would work best for which bits. Then read through the psalm a second time and ask them to make the sounds. On the third or fourth time, you could video yourselves as you read and your child adds musical accompaniment.

QUESTIONS TO ASK ...

Can you name some of the different ways in which we are encouraged to worship God, in this psalm?

Why do you think we often use songs and music?

Why do you think God wants us to worship him?

How can we worship God when we are in a bad mood and life is tough?

A THOUGHT TO PONDER

Our English word 'worship' comes from the Anglo-Saxon 'worth-ship' meaning bringing something of worth to God. Worship is more than singing, it is offering God our whole lives. Worship is a response to all that God is, all that God has, and all that he is doing.

LET'S PRAY

Can you think of everything that you are thankful to God for today? You could write it in a list or take it in turns with your child to name things, perhaps giving a high five for every idea.

In this psalm, the writer talks about us being like sheep. When Jesus comes, he talks about being the Good Shepherd. Ultimately, we can thank God for his son Jesus and his shepherd-like care for us.

If you have actual instruments at home, then why not add them into the mix?

There are also a whole host of other instruments you can make at home. If you've nailed these instruments, then go and create some more!

TOP TIPS

AGE RANGE: 3-7
EFFORT LEVEL: 2/5
TIMING: 40 MINS
VITAL EQUIPMENT: VARIOUS CRAFT MATERIALS

ADVENTURE 36
Chain Reaction

We've all seen the domino effect. One domino topples, knocking down the next, then the next and so on. The aim of this adventure is to create a chain reaction around your house that ends by fulfilling an everyday task. So when you nudge the first thing, it sets off a chain reaction around the house and finishes by doing something like turning the light switch on!

WHAT YOU DO:

1. The first thing to do is to get inspired. It was the engineer and cartoonist Rube Goldberg who first made these chain reaction ideas popular. If you search for his name on YouTube, you will find lots of videos to give you ideas.

2. Once you're feeling inspired, find a simple problem to solve. For example, your chain reaction could end by ringing a bell, blowing out a candle or putting the kettle on.

3. Once you've settled on the problem, it's time to gather some supplies with which to build your contraptions. These could include:
    - Things that roll, such as balls and marbles, skateboards and toy cars
    - Things that fall, such as dominoes but also books, DVD cases and wooden blocks.
    - Things that are powered, such as toasters and fans.
    - Things that build routes, such as tubes, cardboard ramps, pipes and marble runs.
    - Things that hold tension, such as balloons and thread.

4. Lay out all of your material and then go ahead with setting up your chain reaction. Do remember that if your child is young, you can keep this really simple!

BIBLE TO SHARE
1 TIMOTHY 4:12 (Bible Overview 7)

Paul mentored Timothy and sent him on a mission to Ephesus to confront some church leaders on their inconsistent and dangerous teaching. Timothy was still young and might have been expecting that older people in the Ephesian church would not take him seriously. Paul both encourages and challenges him with this verse:

'Don't let anyone look down on you because you are young, but set an example for the believers in speech, in conduct, in love, in faith and in purity.'

QUESTIONS TO ASK ...

In what ways did actions cause reactions in your chain reaction adventure?

Can you think of times when an action causes a reaction in the way we live? (Such as a kind gesture?)

In what ways may older people not take younger people seriously? How do you think Timothy coped?

Thinking about our speech and conduct, how can the way we live have a positive impact on people around us?

A THOUGHT TO PONDER

The Church is ever only a generation from extinction. We learn in Paul's letters that Timothy's faith has been nurtured by his grandmother Lois and his mother Eunice (2 Timothy 1:5).

LET'S PRAY

Think through the past week. Are there moments when you have acted in a certain way and it has had negative reactions? Is there something here to say sorry to God for? Then think through moments when you have acted in a certain way and it has had a positive reaction. Spend a moment thanking God for these moments and asking for more in the coming week.

TOP TIPS

It's always best to start small and add contraptions one at a time. Success will keep your child enthusiastic.

Some contraptions will fail, and that's OK. Remember that it's part of the learning process and an opportunity to help your child think through ideas.

AGE RANGE: 3+
EFFORT LEVEL: 3/5
TIMING: 30-90 MINS
VITAL EQUIPMENT:
VARIOUS HOUSEHOLD ITEMS

ADVENTURE 37

Time Capsule

How will the world be different in 10, 20, or even 50 years' time? This adventure is about creating a time capsule, which will be like a message to the future! Together you will each contribute a couple of items in an airtight container, which might one day be found by people who are not yet born!

WHAT YOU DO:

1. **What goes in?** You want to give the person who discovers your capsule some idea of what it is like to be alive today. You might like to include: a shopping receipt, a cinema ticket, an old toy, some coins, a football match programme.

   It's a good idea to include a letter, written with a permanent marker, with some information about yourselves and perhaps even a reason why you are burying the capsule. Include something about your faith. You might also like to include a prediction for the future, a prayer and even a photograph. It's important that you include the date you put your capsule together.

   It's a good idea to put all organic materials (such as paper) in their own plastic bags for extra protection. You could also laminate your letter if you have a laminator at home.

   It's also important to think about what *doesn't* go in. Food will go stale, tech can become obsolete (just think about the floppy disk!) and bottled drinks can explode and leak.

2. **What kind of container?** You need an airtight aluminium or stainless-steel container if you're hoping that your capsule will stand the test of time. Seal the capsule inside a plastic bag or wrapping to give it extra protection from the elements.

3. **Where to bury it?** Traditionally people have buried time capsules underground. If you're going to do so, try to bury it at least three feet down to protect it from big temperature fluctuations. It's best to bury it in a location that is unlikely to be built over. You could instead hide it somewhere in your own house or in a local church building (such as an attic, basement or crypt).

BIBLE TO SHARE
2 KINGS 22:8-13 (Bible Overview 4)

God's people had become two nations and the northern kingdom (Israel) had been conquered by the Assyrians. The southern kingdom had a succession of bad kings but then Josiah came to the throne at the age of eight. When Josiah was grown up, the high priest Hilkiah found the book of God's Law – God's rules and ways for living, probably the Bible book of Deuteronomy – in God's Temple. When this was reported to Josiah, he tore his robes, saying, 'Go and pray to God about what we must do in response to what is written here. God must be angry that our ancestors haven't obeyed a single one of the rules given in this book.' Josiah led the people in obeying the words written in God's law, and this resulted in a massive change across the kingdom.

QUESTIONS TO ASK ...

What do you think things will be like in the future?

When the book was found, Josiah tore his robes (v11). Why do you think he did this?

How do you think our lives would be different if we didn't have the Bible?

How do we make sure the Bible doesn't get lost in the busyness of life?

A THOUGHT TO PONDER

The book in this passage had been lost in the Temple. The people had never thrown it out or discarded it but it had simply been put to one side and forgotten. When the king rediscovers the book, he is passionate that everybody should have access to it. What does this look like in our lives today?

LET'S PRAY

Hold the Bible in your hands and thank God that he has given us this book to know who he is. Pray for whoever opens the capsule, for them to discover the relevance of whatever you have written about God in your letter.

TOP TIPS

If you are going to bury your box somewhere, you could choose to write the GPS coordinates down to find it again in ten years' time, or even write them down in your will.

AGE RANGE: 3+
EFFORT LEVEL: 3/5
TIMING: 60-90 MINS
VITAL EQUIPMENT: STAINLESS STEEL CONTAINER, VARIOUS HOUSEHOLD ITEMS

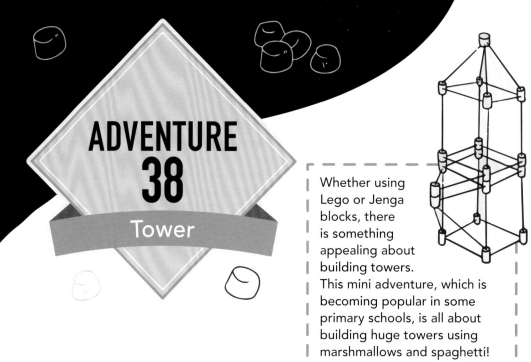

ADVENTURE 38

Tower

Whether using Lego or Jenga blocks, there is something appealing about building towers.
This mini adventure, which is becoming popular in some primary schools, is all about building huge towers using marshmallows and spaghetti!

WHAT YOU DO:

1. With a packet of large marshmallows and a packet of spaghetti, choose your building area. You want a flat surface and I would recommend starting on the floor rather than on the table. The aim is to get the tower as high as possible.

2. The marshmallows become the joins between the spaghetti. Start by snapping a piece of spaghetti in half and using the pieces to build a square with the marshmallows, keeping the pieces of spaghetti adjoined.

3. Next try building the square out into a cube.

4. You'll quickly discover that the cube is quite flimsy. Using some other pieces of spaghetti, broken to the right length, make diagonals across each side of the cube. Your cubes should now be more robust. If you want to make the cube stronger still, you can use several strands of spaghetti for each side.

5. Once you have your first cube built, the challenge now is to build the next cube on top and so on and so on. How high can you make the tower?

6. To top the tower, you could now build a pyramid. Alternatively, you could lay a piece of cardboard down and take it in turns to add weights to the top, to see who makes it come crashing down!

7. If you're keen to go again, you could try to build a bridge, perhaps from the coffee table to the sofa. You can also try using different shapes.

BIBLE TO SHARE
GENESIS 11:1-9 (Bible Overview 1)

After the flood, Noah and his descendants were told to be fruitful and increase in number across the earth. At this time, everyone spoke the same language. As they settled on the plains of Shinar, they said to themselves, 'Let's make a tower that reaches heaven, so that we can be famous.' So they began to build a tower out of bricks and mortar, higher than any building ever before. God was not pleased with this, and he confused their languages so that suddenly they were all speaking in different languages. Because they couldn't communicate, they could not finish building the tower.

QUESTIONS TO ASK ...

Why do you think we like building big towers?

The people wanted to build a tower that reached the heavens and to make a name for themselves. Why do you think God was upset by this plan?

Perhaps the tower symbolised their independence from God. What does it mean to depend on God?

God doesn't send another flood but confuses their languages. Why do you think God did this?

A THOUGHT TO PONDER

New inventions can change how we do life. In this story, the new invention is the brick. It's much easier building with bricks that stack than building with stones that are all different shapes. In what ways can we rely on our own skills and the latest tech rather than looking to God?

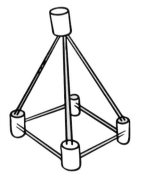

CONTINUED →

LET'S PRAY

Father God, thank you for the gift of building things. Thank you for ideas and creativity. Help us never to become so focused on what we are building that we forget you. May we be more bothered about making your name famous than our own. Amen

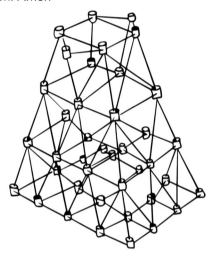

If the pasta and the marshmallows have been on the floor, it might not be very hygienic to eat them!

If you have a microwave, then when you have a marshmallow packet open, you could try this little experiment: keep one marshmallow as a test but then microwave four others: one for 10 seconds, one for 25 seconds, one for 40 seconds and one for 55 seconds. Ask your child to make observations. The science is that the volume of gas in the marshmallow increases when the temperature increases, and then decreases as it cools down. Once they've cooled down, they are edible!

TOP TIPS

AGE RANGE: 5+
EFFORT LEVEL: 1/5
TIMING: 20-40 MINS
VITAL EQUIPMENT: PACK OF SPAGHETTI
PACKET OF LARGE MARSHMALLOWS

ADVENTURE 39

The Circuit

There are some rainy days when my children have too much energy and 'the circuit' is a great way to tire them out! It's basically an indoor mini Olympics, where every room has a challenge to complete and the only question is how effectively your child can do it! You can score each activity, coming up with your own system of scoring and maybe prizes! If you want to really go to town, your child can make signs for each room.

Here are my suggestions:

1. **Shark Run** – Place three pieces of newspaper on the floor. Your child has to cross the room and come back but they can only touch the paper, and they must always have a part of their body touching each piece. They can move the pieces of paper as they go along, but if at any point they are not in contact with a piece, you take it away!

2. **The Floor is Lava** – Very simply, you pretend the floor is lava and your child has to get around the room solely by climbing on furniture. It's important you do a health and safety check on this first as some cupboards can topple and some furniture may not be able to take their weight.

3. **Crab Corridor** – With their back facing the floor, they support themselves on their hands and feet. How many times can they go up and down the corridor in two minutes?

CONTINUED →

4. **Bath Bobsleigh** – You can find videos on YouTube of bobsleigh teams going down a run with a camera on the front. The child has to sit in the (empty) bath with the screen in front and see how accurately they can move their body according to every turn. You might like to have them in a cycle helmet for extra fun!

5. **The Gaffer Wiggle** – Make sure your child is wearing a long sleeve top and leggings or trousers. Gaffer-tape their ankles and their wrists together and set them a challenge to wriggle around the room – perhaps over a bed or under a table.

6. **The Knock Down** – Lay out between five and eight plastic cups on the floor upside down. Take one large pair of ladies' tights (an old pair that can be damaged) and put a tennis ball in the very end. Then put the tights over the child's head (like a bank robber) so that they have the ball dangling down. Your child then has to swing the ball around without using their arms to knock down the cups. How quickly can they do it?

7. **Teddy Bucket** – Line up all the teddies (or balls) in the house that you can find and place a bucket or kitchen bowl a reasonable distance away from your child. How many teddies can they throw into the bucket?

8. **Jumping Jacks** – Give your child two minutes to jump over as many things as they can in one room. Each item they take and jump over, they must return to its place before they take out the second item. For example, they could take a pair of socks out of a drawer, jump over them and then put them back. Then they could take a toy car off the shelf, jump over it, and then return it to the shelf.

9. **Balloon Up** – See how long your child can keep a balloon in the air. If they are older, then bar them from using their hands.

BIBLE TO SHARE
1 CORINTHIANS 12:12-27 (Bible Overview 7)

Paul writes to the church in Corinth who are having various problems. In this chapter, Paul is addressing the issues they have in their worship gatherings. He uses the metaphor (word-picture) of the human body to help his readers understand how they should co-operate with one another, each having different jobs but being part of a greater whole. For example, Paul says, the human body isn't all one gigantic hand or eye, so we don't have to all be the same to be part of the church. Nor is one part more important than the other – you can't imagine your head telling your foot 'I don't need you', can you? You need both for a fully functional body, and Paul says that we need each other in the same way as part of God's family, the church.

QUESTIONS TO ASK ...

Which activity was the hardest?

How do you find it when you can't use certain parts of your body?

Paul describes the church as a body. What part of the body do you think you are most like? Why?

What gifts do you have to serve the church?

A THOUGHT TO PONDER

It's easy to spend our lives comparing ourselves to others. Paul makes it clear that we all have different roles to play and that we are all needed. Who can you think of in your church community that you can encourage in their gifting? Could you perhaps send them an encouraging text or card?

LET'S PRAY

Spend a couple of minutes thinking about some people at church. How are they a gift to the church? Say thanks to God for them and the gifts he has given them.

TOP TIPS

You could make the kitchen the refreshment station whereby your child can nip in to get a drink between activities.

AGE RANGE: 3+
EFFORT LEVEL: 3/5
TIMING: 45-60 MINS
VITAL EQUIPMENT: VARIOUS HOUSEHOLD ITEMS

SECTION 4

EVERYDAY ADVENTURES

As a child, everything is new. So often I take for granted the smell of
autumn or the sound of the train thundering past. They become just part of
the noise of life. As we move through the motions of the day, we can easily
forget that for our children there are a hundred new experiences. What
happens when we slow down to savour the moment? These adventures
may seem like chores to get through, but it's exciting to discover what
happens when we reframe them as everyday adventures and look for what
we can help our children discover about God in the process.

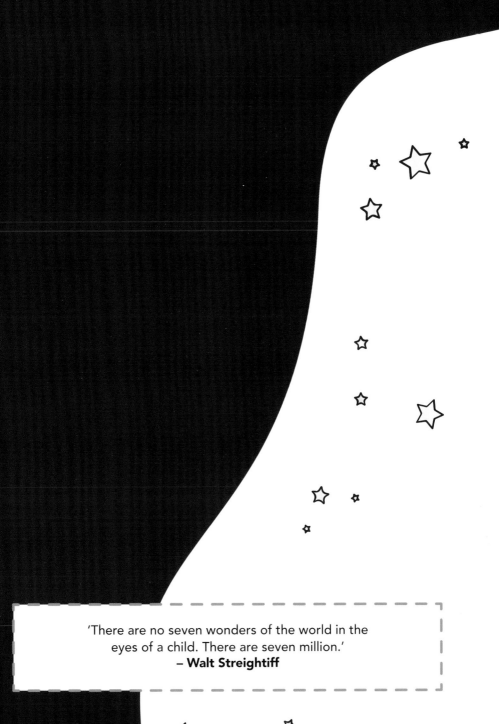

'There are no seven wonders of the world in the eyes of a child. There are seven million.'
– Walt Streightiff

ADVENTURE 40
Car Washing

Helping my dad wash the car was always a fun experience growing up. This is your opportunity to get a chore done whilst also spending some quality time with your child, and potentially having a water fight! You'll probably already have a plan for car washing but below are a few ideas.

WHAT YOU DO:

1. Get your supplies ready! (See the list overleaf.)

2. Get dressed in appropriate car-cleaning clothes and make sure the car is in a safe place for your child to help clean it. Make sure the windows are up and the windscreen wipers are away from the glass.

3. Ideally, if you have a hose, give the car a quick once-over first to remove any debris. It's best to aim the water jet downwards on surfaces, so that the dirty water runs off.

4. Get your car-washing gloves, soak them in the soapy water and then start scrubbing the surface of your car, moving from section to section, and working from top to bottom. Remember to keep rinsing the glove through. Use the other bucket of water to rinse down the area you have washed and if you have a hose, then hose down each section before you move on to scrubbing the next.

5. Don't forget the mirrors, the windows and the door shuts. You will need to open the doors briefly to clean the door shuts (the metal strips inside the door well).

6. Get your bucket of warm water with detergent and finish by washing the wheels. These will be the dirtiest part of the car. You might want to use a plastic brush with stiff bristles to clean the dirt from your tyre sidewalls.

7. Dry the car properly with microfibre drying cloths or towels. Just before you start drying, you may find that some sections of the car are already getting dry. If that is the case, give them another quick spray with the hose. When you're finished using the drying cloths, pop them in the washing machine, ready for next time.

8. Finally, if you're going all out, use car wax and/or car polish and a microfibre cloth for the perfect finishing touch. This will help protect the paint from the sun.

BIBLE TO SHARE
JOHN 13:12-17 (Bible Overview 6)

Jesus enjoyed a final meal with his disciples before he was arrested and went to the cross. During the meal, he washed his disciples' feet. He said to them, 'Do you understand what I have done for you? You call me 'Master' and 'Teacher' and this is right, for so I am. So if I, your Master and Teacher, have washed your feet, so you ought to wash one another's feet. I've laid down a pattern for you to follow.'

As you read this story, you might like to use the bucket to wash your child's feet or invite them to wash yours!

QUESTIONS TO ASK ...

Why do you think the disciples needed their feet washing?

How do you think it feels having someone wash your feet? Do you think it tickles?

Can you imagine a king or queen washing your feet? Can you imagine Jesus washing your feet?

Why do you think Jesus did this?

A THOUGHT TO PONDER

Jesus is often described as the Servant King. In this story, although it is acknowledged that he is Lord, Jesus performs the job of the servant, washing feet that would have walked many miles on some pretty filthy roads. Jesus then commands the disciples to wash each other's feet. We don't normally wash each other's feet in this day and age, so what might we do instead?

CONTINUED →

LET'S PRAY

Think about the ways God serves us today and thank him for each of them.

If you don't own a car, is there somebody who would appreciate you washing their car for them?

Cleaning a car is hard work, so keep it fun with lots of laughter.

Remember not to use the plastic brush on the body of the car as it can leave scratch marks.

AGE RANGE: 3+
EFFORT LEVEL: 4/5
TIMING: 60 MINS
VITAL EQUIPMENT: CAR WASH DETERGENT, ONE BUCKET WITH WARM WATER AND CORRECT WATER-TO-DETERGENT RATIO ONE BUCKET WITH WARM CLEAN WATER FOR RINSING A HOSE (IF POSSIBLE), MICROFIBRE CLOTHS OR TOWELS FOR DRYING, TWO WASHING GLOVES EACH, PLASTIC BRUSH FOR THE TYRE SIDEWALLS, WAX OR POLISH (OPTIONAL)

ADVENTURE 41

Story Time

When we do story time at home, it can often be the means by which we calm our child down, ready for bed. But if you are doing a story time in the middle of the day, then make it an everyday adventure by acting out a story from the Gospels.

WHAT YOU DO:

1. First up, you need to build a boat! You could pull two sofas or a bed into the centre of the room. Every boat needs a sail and using a sheet, a broom and some tape, create your mast and sail. If your child is younger, you might like to bring various cuddly toys aboard to be some of the disciples.

2. Now take each line of the story from the reading below and act it out.

3. Verse 35: Ask your child to imagine what the day has been like. How do you think the disciples were feeling?

4. Verse 36: Climb aboard the boat and say goodbye to those staying on land.

5. Verse 37: Make the sounds of the storm, getting louder and louder – think wind, rain, and thunder! For dramatic effect, you could also go and wet your face under the tap, to give yourself that drenched look.

6. Verse 38: Using a cushion, one of you now pretends to be Jesus. Was he a snorer? The other one wakes Jesus up. Did he do it quietly and discreetly, or not?

7. Verse 39: Whilst one of you makes the noise of the storm, the other one says the words of Jesus. The storm noises stop.

8. Verse 40: Jesus asks his questions.

9. Verse 41: The one playing the disciple acts terrified!

10. Having acted it out once, you might like to go again, changing roles. You might even like to perform it to family members later!

CONTINUED →

BIBLE TO SHARE
MARK 4:35-41 (Bible Overview 6)

One evening by the side of a great lake, Jesus said to his disciples 'Let's go across to the other side.' Leaving the crowd of people on that side, they all got into the boat. A great storm blew in, and the waves began crashing into the boat so that it filled with water. But Jesus was in the back of the boat, sleeping on a cushion. The disciples woke him up, saying, 'Teacher, we're going to die! Don't you care?' Jesus woke up and said to the wind and waves, 'Peace! Be still!' Immediately the wind and waves stopped, and everything was calm. Jesus then said to the disciples, 'Why are you so afraid? Do you still have no faith in me?' They were filled with fear and said to one another, 'Who is this, that even the wind and waves obey him?'

QUESTIONS TO ASK ...

What is the silliest question you've heard?

Jesus asked his friends, 'Why are you so afraid?' Why was this a silly question to them?

Could it have been that Jesus asked the question for the disciples' benefit more than his?

What different emotions do you think the disciples experienced in this story?

A THOUGHT TO PONDER

We all experience storms in life – hard times, sickness, things not going our way. Sometimes Jesus does the miraculous and calms the storms, but sometimes he doesn't. It's in these times, when we don't always understand what Jesus is doing, that we can remember that he is with us.

LET'S PRAY

Lie quietly in your boat and play a worship song on your phone or a CD player and 'soak' in God's presence, asking that you would know God is with you no matter what storms you face.

You can try this way of acting out Bible stories with other favourites, such as Noah's Ark, David and Goliath (try acting as Goliath with a child on your shoulders!), the paralysed man being lowered through the roof and the parable of the Good Samaritan.

TOP TIPS

AGE RANGE: 3+
EFFORT LEVEL: 2/5
TIMING: 20-40 MINS
VITAL EQUIPMENT: SHEET, BROOM OR MOP STICK, FURNITURE, CUSHION MUSIC PLAYER TO PLAY A WORSHIP SONG

ADVENTURE 42

Chore-tastic Relay

One of my daily challenges is trying to get my kids to help with chores – anything from unloading the dishwasher to putting their clothes away. Here are five ideas for turning chores into a mini adventure.

WHAT YOU DO:

1. Hovering Hoovers! Try to hoover an entire room without your child touching the floor.

2. Dress up, no mess up! Get yourself and your child dressed up in fancy dress. Then tidy up in the style of your outfit. For example, how would a superhero put toys away? How would a lion wash up?

3. Musical Scrubbing! Whether you are scrubbing the bath or the stairs, take the necessary cleaning equipment and with a song blaring, race to clean your target before the music stops.

4. Charade-Away! Turn the simple job of putting clothes away into a little game by challenging your child to put each piece of clothing away as a different character or animal. Your job is to guess who they are pretending to be.

5. Bottom Mop! If you have lino in your home, then set your child up with a cloth under their bottom and see how quickly they can clean the floor by moving around the floor.

BIBLE TO SHARE

1 SAMUEL 16:4-13 (Bible Overview 3)

This story is set when Israel had Saul as their king. Saul had become proud and the prophet Samuel was sent to anoint a new king. He went to the house of a man named Jesse, who had many sons. Samuel met seven of Jesse's sons, but it was clear to him that God had not chosen any of them to be king. So Jesse called in his youngest son, David, who had been looking after sheep in the field. He was handsome and cheerful, and God said to Samuel, 'This is the one.' So Samuel anointed David with oil, and David was filled with the Holy Spirit.

In this story, Samuel discovered that he should not look at the outward appearance because God looks at the heart. The oil anointing was a symbolic act that David would be king.

QUESTIONS TO ASK ...

What kind of attitude do we normally have about chores?

When a job doesn't look fun and we're asked to help, what do we sometimes do?

What do you think a king or queen should look like? What matters more, how a king or queen looks or how they act?

What do you think it means for us to have a heart after God?

A THOUGHT TO PONDER

Samuel explains that David is a man after God's heart (1 Samuel 13:14). Even as a young boy, David had this attribute. In his life, he was far from perfect but he was humble before God and faithful to God. What might these characteristics look like in our lives?

LET'S PRAY

This may be an opportunity to say sorry to God for the times we have had the wrong attitude in our hearts. It might be that you, as the dad, want to start by sharing some way in which you have had the wrong heart attitude. David prays 'Create in me a clean heart' (Psalm 51:10). Maybe you could pray that together.

If this works, this might become a regular adventure. What better way to tackle chores?!

TOP TIPS

AGE RANGE: 3-7
EFFORT LEVEL: 1/5
TIMING: 20-40 MINS
VITAL EQUIPMENT: CLEANING EQUIPMENT, MUSIC

ADVENTURE 43

The Adventure Dinner Party

Often adventures mean travel and trying out new things. Over the years I have had the privilege of travelling to many different countries and love to tell my kids stories of how I have eaten snakes, rats, and insects. This adventure is one of both the taste buds and the imagination!

WHAT YOU DO:

1. First up, introduce the idea of hosting an adventure dinner party. Are there some other members of the family that you could make tea for?

2. To get the ball rolling, blindfold your child and then give them a taste test. When you spoon-feed them, can they work out from the taste what it is? You could try jam, peanut butter, a coffee granule, horseradish or raisins. If that's too easy, try some of the herbs. (Have a glass of water on hand and be aware of allergies.)

3. Now for the cooking. You are going to make a two course adventure feast: Eyeball Tomato Soup and Worm-infested Apple.

   Get the ingredients together for the soup (see overleaf). Start by melting the butter over a medium heat in a large saucepan. Cut the onion into quarters and cut the tomatoes into quarters. Tip them into the saucepan alongside the water and stock and a teaspoon of salt.

   Bring the soup to a simmer and keep cooking it for about 40 minutes, stirring it occasionally. Taste to see if it needs a touch more salt. You may also like to add a small handful of basil. Once it's cooked, pour it into a blender and get blending. Depending on the size of your blender, you might need to do this a bit at a time.

   For the eyeballs, take the mozzarella balls and slice them thinly. Then take the black olives and cut them in half. Using your creative flair, place the slices of the black olives in the centre of the mozzarella. You now have some eyeballs.

Once the soup is blended, reheat and serve, with the eyeballs placed delicately on top, so that they float.

Serve with bread.

For the worm-infested apples, simply take an apple corer (or a sharp knife) and cut a hole in the top of the apple. Then squeeze multiple sweetie worms into the gap so that it looks like they are escaping from the top of the apple!

Serve to your guests.

4. If your child is a little older, then whilst they are preparing the soup, you might like to give them an opportunity to try some different ingredients from around the world. They could sample biltong, dates, seaweed or stuffed vine leaves.

5. If there is time, why not go all out and encourage your child to make place mats, name holders and even a branded restaurant sign and menu? They could even dress up as a waiter or waitress.

BIBLE TO SHARE

PSALM 34:8 (Bible Overview 3)

Before David was King of Israel, he had a whole host of challenges. As a musician he wrote lots of psalms to help us come to God at different times of our lives. In Psalm 34, the first section (verses 1-10) is about praising God and sharing testimony. The second section (verses 11-22) is the instruction that flows from that experience. Tucked in the first section is this beautiful verse:

'Taste and see that the Lord is good;
blessed is the one who takes refuge in him.'

QUESTIONS TO ASK ...

What are your favourite things to eat?

Why do you think David uses the words 'taste and see' when we can't eat God, or see him like we see other people?

How might you have experienced God?

I wonder what it means to take refuge in God?

CONTINUED →

A THOUGHT TO PONDER

David used song and poetry to express his relationship with God. How do we express our relationship with God? Should we think about writing or painting our experiences of God?

LET'S PRAY

Write (or draw) your own prayer or psalm like David. You might like to think about the different senses of sight, smell, taste, sound and touch as ways of thinking about how we connect with God.

TOP TIPS

Be careful when cooking the soup and pouring it, that your child doesn't get burnt.

AGE RANGE: 3+
EFFORT LEVEL: 4/5
TIMING: 60-90 MINS
VITAL EQUIPMENT: SEE BELOW

EYEBALL TOMATO SOUP (SERVES 4)
8 TABLESPOONS OF UNSALTED BUTTER
ONE LARGE ONION
22 MEDIUM TOMATOES
MOZZARELLA BALLS
BLACK OLIVES
3 CUPS WATER WITH 2 CUBES OF
VEGETABLE OR CHICKEN STOCK
1 TEASPOON SEA SALT
BREAD, TO SERVE (OPTIONAL)
A BLENDER

WORM-INFESTED APPLES
ONE APPLE PER GUEST
4-5 SWEETIE WORMS PER APPLE

DIFFERENT INGREDIENTS FROM AROUND THE WORLD (OPTIONAL)

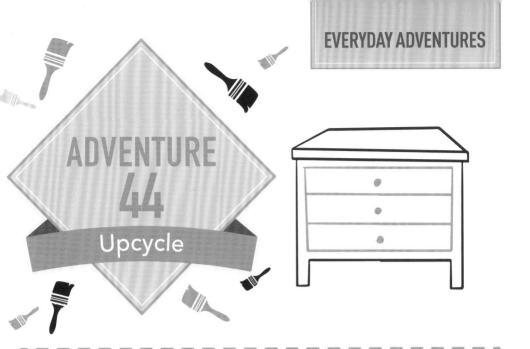

ADVENTURE 44
Upcycle

As kids grow up, we are continually sorting out bedrooms as cots are replaced with child beds and drawers are replaced with wardrobes. This is an opportunity to have a go at upcycling a piece of furniture!

WHAT YOU DO:

1. The first thing you need is something to upcycle. If you have nothing at home, check out your local charity shop or a website like Gumtree. It could be an old jewellery box, a bedside table or even a chair. Alternatively, you could get creative and turn something like an old wooden ladder into a plant display stand or a bookcase, giving an old item a new purpose.

2. Help your child capture a vision for your piece of furniture. Use your imagination, get some ideas online and remember to bear in mind the original style. It's also helpful to think through where the piece of furniture will live afterwards. Which room will it be in, or will it be sold on?

3. Head down to the local DIY shop and stock up on necessary supplies. You'll probably need some paint and if your piece of furniture has old handles, why not splash out on some new ones?

4. It's important that you have all the necessary tools and equipment laid out. Give your chosen piece of furniture a wipe down first, and set up your decorating area with plenty of fresh air and covers to protect the floor.

CONTINUED →

A few things to remember:
- Sand down pieces of furniture before you give them a fresh coat of paint.
- If your piece has knobs or handles, remove them first so you don't attach new ones only to find that they are smaller and there are spaces with no paint!
- Where possible, protect your upcycled furniture with wax or varnish to keep it safe.
- You can try using wallpaper or stencils.

BIBLE TO SHARE

ACTS 9:1-9 (Bible Overview 7)

Once Jesus had gone back to heaven, the Holy Spirit arrived at Pentecost and the church grew hugely, but there were many who did not like this new Jesus movement taking hold and disrupting things. The church began to be persecuted (this means that the enemies of God's church used violence against Christians or locked them up). A man named Saul was a keen persecutor of Christians, and was present at the death of Stephen in Acts 8:1. But on his way to the city of Damascus to persecute more Christians, a light from heaven flashed around him and he fell to the ground. He heard a voice saying, 'Saul, Saul, why are you being so cruel to me?'

'Who are you, Lord?' Saul asked. 'I am Jesus, the one whom you are hurting,' came the reply. 'Now get up and go into the city; you will be told what you must do.' So Saul got up, but he was now blind; the men travelling with him had to lead him by the hand into Damascus. For three days he ate nothing and saw nothing, until God healed him through a man named Ananias, and called Saul to his service.

Saul, who was later renamed Paul, went on to be arguably the greatest missionary that ever lived, writing much of the New Testament.

QUESTIONS TO ASK ...

How difficult was it to transform the piece of furniture?

How hard do you think it is to transform a person's life like Saul?

Why do you think Jesus spoke to him so clearly?

The Bible doesn't say what happened to the men with Saul. What do you think might have happened to them?

A THOUGHT TO PONDER

In the vision, Jesus says to Saul, 'Why are you being so cruel to me?' Saul wasn't being cruel to Jesus directly but to his people, the church. Why do you think Jesus spoke these words?

LET'S PRAY

Who seems very far from God right now?
How might you pray for them?

Start with something simple when upcycling and see how your child gets on. If they enjoy it, you can always go for a bigger, more complicated piece next time!

TOP TIPS

AGE RANGE: 3+
EFFORT LEVEL: 4/5
TIMING: 90-120 MINS
VITAL EQUIPMENT: A PIECE OF FURNITURE, THE NECESSARY RESOURCES TO TRANSFORM YOUR CHOSEN ITEM

ADVENTURE 45

Power Down

Have you ever had a power cut? As a child, I remember the excitement when suddenly the power went out. This adventure, which works best in the winter months, is about turning off the power for an evening and surviving without any screens! Once you've hit the lights, here are some ideas of things that you can do without electricity.

WHAT YOU DO:

1. Have a go at doing ordinary things in the dark – things like tying your shoelaces, drawing a picture and eating a bowl of cereal.

2. Get out a torch and practice making shadow puppets with your hands. (If you have a quick look on the internet beforehand, you can find out how to use your hands to make the shape of various animals.)

3. Play hide and seek with a torch! It's just like playing the normal game except that when you've been flashed with the torch, you've been found.

4. If you have glow sticks, you can attach them to your child with safety pins, along the arms and the legs, so that you create a stick man. Then film them with your smartphone with some music on and you create a brilliant stick man dancing!

5. When it's time for bed, share a candlelit story. I regularly give my kids candlelit stories, with the candle held carefully beneath my face, casting shadows. Ask your child to blow the candle out at the end.

BIBLE TO SHARE

PSALM 23 (Bible Overview 3)

Psalm 23 was written by King David and begins with three verses that depict a serene country walk with green pastures, quiet waters and straight paths. Then verse four changes tack and begins talking about the darkest of valleys. And in verse five, we have this strange picture of a meal prepared whilst surrounded by enemies. The final verse reminds us that God's love is always with us.

QUESTIONS TO ASK ...

How would life be different if there was never electricity again?

How would you cope with no light in the evenings?

I wonder why David did not fear when he knew God was with him?

How might God comfort us in the difficult times of life?

A THOUGHT TO PONDER

Circumstances change. In our lives there will probably be times where we feel like we are in green pastures, and there will probably be some moments that feel like dark valleys. The danger is that too often, our feelings are dictated by our circumstances rather than by God.

In Psalm 23:5, although enemies surround David, God has laid out a banquet for him. In this verse we see that even in dark moments with the enemy all around, God is present, meeting David's needs.

LET'S PRAY

Read the words of Psalm 23:1-5 slowly, ideally with the light from a candle flickering.

If you are going to turn off the lights at the fuse box, make sure you don't inadvertently turn off the fridge and freezer!

AGE RANGE: 3+
EFFORT LEVEL: 4/5
TIMING: 90-120 MINS
VITAL EQUIPMENT: VARIOUS
HOUSEHOLD ITEMS

ADVENTURE 46

Shopping List

I used to love watching Supermarket Sweep as a kid. Going to the supermarket can seem like just another chore to get through, but it can easily become an adventurous game. The simple idea is that your child is given the shopping list and has to go around the shop quickly, carefully collecting everything that is needed. Oh … and it's against the clock!

WHAT YOU DO:

1. First, write out the shopping list on a piece of paper. You might like to attach it to a clipboard and to add a pen, so that your child can tick off each item as they collect it.

2. Get a trolley for your child and give them the list. Explain what they have to do. If they are young, you will need to stay next to them the entire time. If they are slightly older, watch them at a distance and see how they get on. When they set off, try not to interfere too much and remember to make sure there is somewhere to meet just in case you get separated.

3. Depending on the age of your child, you might like to make it more complicated by giving them a budget and asking them to keep tabs on how much the shop will cost.

4. When the rules are understood, start a timer on your phone – giving them a time limit to try and complete the shop!

5. When they finish and arrive at the checkout counter, you might like to mark how they got on. Perhaps a point for each item that is perfect and a point taken off for every mistake.

6. Once the challenge is complete, why not stop for a celebratory coffee and chat through the Bible story?

BIBLE TO SHARE

MATTHEW 28:17-20 (Bible Overview 6)

The Great Commission, as it is called, is Jesus' instruction to his disciples after he has been raised from the dead. He first appeared to Mary in the garden, then a few times to the disciples in the locked room and he appeared at Lake Galilee to have a breakfast barbecue with the disciples and a chat with Peter in particular.

As they gathered on a mountain top, the disciples worshipped but some still doubted. The commission was given to them all. Jesus told them, 'Go and tell everyone, in every nation, about me. Baptise them in the name of the Father, the Son, and the Holy Spirit, and then teach them to obey all that I have commanded you. And surely I will be with you always, even to the very end of the age.'

QUESTIONS TO ASK ...

What was it like being sent with the shopping list? How did you feel about the task you had been given?

How do you think the disciples felt when they were told to go and make disciples of 'all nations'?

What do you think it means to be a disciple of Jesus today?

How can we share the things Jesus taught with others?

A THOUGHT TO PONDER

Jesus' promise could have just been, 'I am with you', but he says, 'And surely I am with you always, to the very end of the age.'

No matter what we go through, he makes it absolutely clear that he is with us.

LET'S PRAY

Where might God be asking us to share about his love? Pray that you would carry his message wherever you go.

If you have more than one child, they can either work as a team or, if they're old enough, they might like to compete with different lists.

Remember that young children may need help with products on high shelves. If your child is really young, you could try a limited version of this adventure by giving them items per aisle.

TOP TIPS

AGE RANGE: 5+
EFFORT LEVEL: 1/5
TIMING: 30 MINS
VITAL EQUIPMENT: SHOPPING LIST
SUPERMARKET

ADVENTURE 47
Stargazing

I live in London where the light pollution is pretty bad, but even in my garden you can see a couple of stars and the odd satellite going by. If you live in a more isolated spot, this is a chance to kick back and watch the night sky, perhaps with a hot chocolate in hand. Hammocks have provided safe sleeping for explorers in swamps and jungles when they didn't fancy sharing their sleeping bag with spiders, scorpions and snakes!

WHAT YOU DO:

1. You need a large sheet of tarpaulin. (Note that you could instead use a sheet of nylon, but linen bed sheets rip or tear too easily.) The sheet needs to be roughly 3 to 3.5 metres by 1.5 metres.

2. Unfold the sheet and flatten it on the floor.

3. Start at one of the long sides of the sheet and roll it up until the middle. Then go to the other side and do the same, so that you meet the other roll. It should now look like you have two snakes lying side by side.

4. Go to one of the ends and bend the two rolls of tarp in the same direction so that it makes the shape of a J at the end. You are now going to tie the first length of rope to the end using a double sheet bend. It might help to watch a YouTube video of this first. Pull it tight.

5. Now do the same at the other end with the other length of rope.

6. Next, tie the ropes as high as you can reach to trees, so that your hammock is nicely lifted off the floor. The trees should be at least leg-thick. If there are no trees present (like in our garden), then you can fix the hammock to something else that is sturdy such as a fence pillar (using a c-clamp) or by screwing an eye-screw into your wall. Note that both the tarp and the rope will stretch a bit and you want to be at least a couple of feet off the ground.

7. Before lying on your hammock, test it by gently sitting on it first.

BIBLE TO SHARE
GENESIS 15:5 (Bible Overview 1)

Abram, a follower of God, was an old man. He had no children of his own and yet God made him a promise, telling Abram to go outside of the tent he lived in and look up at the stars. 'Do you see how many there are? Can you count them? You are going to have far more descendants than there are stars in the sky.' This seemed impossible to Abram, but God was quite serious!

QUESTIONS TO ASK ...

How many stars can you see at night?

How do you think Abram felt about being given this promise?

What promises has God made to us?

How can we know his promises are true?

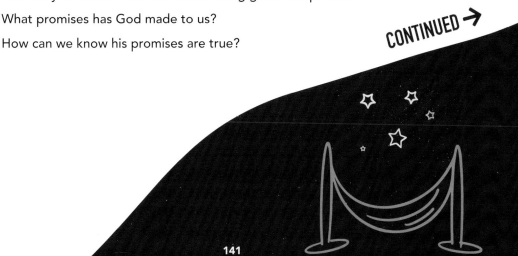

CONTINUED →

141

A THOUGHT TO PONDER

God goes on in Chapter 15 to ask Abram to make a covenant with a ceremony involving dead animals. The animals are laid out and according to tradition, a conquered tribe would have to walk the bloody gauntlet as a way of confirming the covenant. Interestingly, God doesn't make Abram walk it but instead a blazing torch, which symbolised God, travels through the bodies. God is showing his commitment to Abram.

LET'S PRAY

What began with Abram now includes you and me. We are part of that promise as we have been adopted into God's family. There are Christians in every country on earth. Ask your child to name as many countries as they can and then say a short prayer for the church in those different nations. Finish by thanking God for his promises.

TOP TIPS

Be careful that the hammock is secure. It is also easy for the occupants to roll out, so take care that your children don't fall out!

AGE RANGE: 3+
EFFORT LEVEL: 3/5
TIMING: 30-40 MINS
VITAL EQUIPMENT: TARPAULIN (3 TO 3.5 METRES BY 1.5 METRES) TWO LENGTHS OF ROPE, TREES OR SOMETHING STURDY TO TIE YOUR HAMMOCK TO, C-CLAMPS OR AN EYE-SCREW (IF NECESSARY)

ADVENTURE 48
Busy Bees

During the summer days, whilst you're spending more time outdoors, why not build a bee hotel for solitary bees that don't live in hives? With bees under threat and yet so important to our existence, creating a bee hotel is a great way to help them thrive again. There are lots of ways to make a bee hotel – we have gone for the simplest!

WHAT YOU DO:

1. Take an empty two-litre plastic bottle. Take off any outer wrappers and carefully cut off both ends so that you end up with a plastic cylinder.

2. Thread a length of twine through the cylinder so that you can hang up the hotel once you have finished.

3. Next, you need to find some nesting tubes. Collect dead stems of hollow plants, bamboo, reeds and twigs. These must all be dry.

4. If you have some large sticks, you can drill holes between 3mm and 5mm wide and up to 10cm deep.

5. Make sure all of the nesting tubes you have found are at least 6cm shorter than the cylinder so that the plastic will protect them from getting wet. You may need to use garden clippers to trim the tubes.

6. Solitary bees don't like sharp edges near entry holes and so, using sandpaper, you may want to sand down the ends.

7. Pack the cylinder with the nesting tubes you have found, making sure they are tightly packed and secure.

8. Finally, set up your bee hotel so that it faces south and will get lots of sun. It should be at least one metre off the ground, fixed firmly to a wall, fence or pillar with nothing blocking the entrances. Ideally it should be near plants and shrubs.

9. Over the coming days, keep checking your hotel to see if any guests have arrived!

CONTINUED →

BIBLE TO SHARE
MARK 11:1-11 (Bible Overview 6)

Jesus and his disciples were going to Jerusalem for the Passover feast. Before they got there, Jesus sent two of his disciples on ahead to get a colt (a young donkey) for him to ride, telling them exactly where they would find it. When they brought it back, the disciples all placed their cloaks over the colt for a saddle and Jesus got on. There were many people lining the way and they spread their cloaks or palm branches over the road. Other people went ahead of Jesus, shouting, 'Hosanna! Blessed is he who comes in the name of the Lord!'

This Palm Sunday story is the beginning of Holy Week as Jesus enters Jerusalem. As you read it, ask your child to imagine the sights, the noise and the smells.

QUESTIONS TO ASK ...

What was it like preparing for the bees to stay?

What do you do to make a friend coming to your home feel welcome?

Why do you think the people wanted to welcome Jesus into Jerusalem?

What do you think it may mean to welcome Jesus into our lives today?

A THOUGHT TO PONDER

The Roman leaders would have entered Jerusalem on a white stallion with soldiers and swords. Jesus enters on a baby donkey with civilians and children and no weapons, just palm leaves. This passage shows both the majesty of Jesus and the humility of Jesus. His Kingdom is not one of fear but one of love.

LET'S PRAY

Imagine Jesus arriving in your town or city. What would you say to him? Make that your prayer today.

Bees need different plants at different times of the year and they also need rain water. If you want to take this adventure further, you can go online and find out what you can plant in the garden to encourage bees to take up residence.

If your bee hotel is successful, you will need to move it into a shed or garage (somewhere dry that isn't heated) from October to early March, to protect any bee eggs inside.

TOP TIPS

Not all bee hotels will work. If you are keen to try again, there are lots more permanent bee hotel ideas online.

AGE RANGE: 4+
EFFORT LEVEL: 4/5
TIMING: 60 MINS
VITAL EQUIPMENT:
PLASTIC TWO-LITRE BOTTLE
TWINE, DRY HOLLOW PLANTS
BAMBOO, REEDS AND TWIGS, SANDPAPER
GARDEN CLIPPERS AND DRILL (OPTIONAL)
SOMEWHERE TO FIX YOUR BEE HOTEL

ADVENTURE 49

Get Lost!

As a family, we are often running late or in such a hurry that we don't have time to explore properly. This is a very simple adventure when you're out and about with some spare time on your hands. You are simply going to take directions from your child.

WHAT YOU DO:

1. Whether you are going by foot, by bike or by car, share the simple rules, that when your child says 'right', you will turn right. When they say 'turn left', you will turn left and when they say 'straight on', you will keep going straight on! (Obviously within the realms of safety!)

2. The object of the adventure is to give your child control and see where you end up. Will you discover somewhere new?

3. The adventure is about discovery. Once your child has grasped the concept, you can go a step further and introduce picture-taking.

4. Try to capture the route you are taking by snapping photos. To make it more interesting, ask your child to take the pictures and if you are on foot, encourage them to take photos from a different viewpoint capturing a unique perspective. For example, they could snap a photo lying underneath a tree or from standing on top of a letter box.

5. The challenge then is to either find a shortcut back to your starting point or to try and retrace your steps back to where you began.

6. With an older child, you could finish by setting them the challenge of trying to draw a map of the route and seeing how accurate it is!

BIBLE TO SHARE

MATTHEW 18:12-14 (Bible Overview 6)

Having placed a little child in front of the disciples and saying that unless they believed in God as readily as a child, they would never enter heaven, Jesus spoke about God's love for us, using the metaphor (word-picture) of sheep and a shepherd.

'What do you think?' he said. 'If a shepherd has a hundred sheep, and one wanders off, won't he leave the ninety-nine where they are and go to look for the lost one? And when he finds it, won't he be happier about that than about the ninety-nine who were never in danger? In the same way, your Father in heaven does not want any of these little ones to be lost.'

In a world that often looked down on children, Jesus taught the disciples that everybody is important to God. One hundred represented an average-sized flock and at this time in history, shepherds would often leave their flock with other shepherds to search after lost sheep.

QUESTIONS TO ASK ...

Why do you think getting lost can be so scary?

I wonder what it would have been like for a shepherd losing one of his sheep? What would you have done?

How do you think we can get lost from God?

How might God find us if we do get lost?

A THOUGHT TO PONDER

Like the shepherd cares for each sheep, God cares for each of us. This story shows God's compassion and how when a lost sheep is found, it makes him happy. As we are called to be God's representatives on earth, how do you think God might want us to be like shepherds, helping lost people come back to God?

LET'S PRAY

There are many phrases to describe Jesus. One is the Good Shepherd. Think about what makes a good shepherd and then thank Jesus for these things.

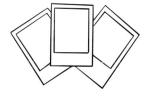

TOP TIPS

Depending on the age of your child, you could do this locally or you could go to a place that none of you are familiar with!

AGE RANGE: 3+
EFFORT LEVEL: 1/5
TIMING: 20-60 MINS
VITAL EQUIPMENT:
SMARTPHONE OR CAMERA

ADVENTURE 50
Carbecue Pilgrimage

A few times a year, we have to take a long journey somewhere. It might be to visit family or to go on holiday. I have done a couple of these trips solo with my kids and we all know that car journeys can be very tedious. So why not turn one into a mini adventure?

WHAT YOU DO:

1. A few days before you set off, research pilgrimage (a journey to a sacred place) locations en route – these could be old abbeys, monasteries, crosses on hillsides or places of spiritual significance. Find out some interesting ideas about your chosen place, so you can retell the story of this place on the way.

2. Before you start the journey, spend a few minutes talking your kids through the different parts of the car. Your child could also help you check the oil and sort the tyre pressure.

3. Why not cook en route? To make the journey extra exciting, tell your child that you are going to cook a meal on the engine – call it a carbecue! Here's what to do:

   - Choose what to cook. We would normally do hot dog sausages on a shorter trip or sweet potatoes on a longer route. (The general rule is that food will cook slower than an oven but faster than a slow cooker.)

   - Prepare the food as if it was going in the oven. Take some aluminium foil, put a little vegetable oil in the layer with the food, and wrap it up tightly. We tend to use three sheets of aluminium foil so that it is nicely secure.

   - Place the food on a cooking surface on your engine that will get hot. If you're not sure where to place it, drive for five minutes first and then lightly touch the engine to find where it will get hot. It needs to be secure and you may be able to place it under rubber casing.

   - When you arrive at your pilgrimage site, turn off the engine first and, using oven gloves, remove the food carefully and enjoy. Note that getting timings right for food does take some trial and error!

4. With your feast in hand, head off to your pilgrimage spot and use the devotional below.

BIBLE TO SHARE

PSALM 121 (Bible Overview 3)

Commentators believe that Psalm 121 pictures a pilgrimage journey to Jerusalem. The journey is hard and dangerous with various perils lying ahead, and the opening line is an acknowledgement of the need for help. The psalmist looks up to the mountains – the place where all kinds of idolatry took place – and there is a sense of wondering and searching. 'Where does my help come from?' As you share this psalm, explain to your child why the place you are walking to has some spiritual significance.

QUESTIONS TO ASK ...

What do you think a pilgrimage is? Why do people go to sacred places?

What do you think were some of the dangers for the people at the time this psalm was written in travelling to Jerusalem?

How does knowing God is watching over you give you comfort?

A THOUGHT TO PONDER

Sometimes we can take this psalm too literally, and believe that following God means there will be no trouble in the journey of life. The truth is, there will be hardships, but despite those difficulties there are echoes of Romans 8:38, that nothing can separate us from God's love. No matter how easy or tough the journey of life is, the psalmist reminds us that our help comes from the Lord, the Maker of heaven and earth.

LET'S PRAY

As you walk to the place you are going to, invite God to journey with you and to make your pilgrimage special.

Car engines get really hot, so do take care.

You can find a variety of carbecue recipes online.

Remember that your pilgrimage destination doesn't have to be anything too grand. It could be a place that is special to you – for example, the church building you attended as a child.

TOP TIPS

AGE RANGE: 3+
EFFORT LEVEL: 4/5
TIMING: 90-120 MINS
VITAL EQUIPMENT: FOOD TO COOK
ALUMINIUM FOIL, A CAR

ADVENTURE 51

Stairway Fundraising

In the winter months, the evenings are dark and it's very easy to sit in front of a screen. This adventure is a challenge to walk up and down the stairs in your house, raising money for a good cause. Here's how it works …

WHAT YOU DO:

1. First, choose a charity or a cause that you want to raise some money for. Ask your child to choose an issue that they are passionate about.

2. Choose a mountain! In the UK, Ben Nevis is the highest at 1,345 metres and Snowdon is the highest in England and Wales at 1,085 metres. These are a good target. Everest is 8,850 metres!

3. Work out how high your stairs are in metres and then work out how many times you would need to walk up the stairs to reach the target. (If you live in a bungalow, then are there some public stairs nearby?)

4. Set up a sponsored giving page and choose:
   - whether you are going to try and ascend the height in a day or a week
   - whether you are going to do it solo or make it a joint effort

5. At the top of the stairs put a picture of your mountain on the wall and at the bottom of the stairs, place a pen and paper to tick off every time you have gone up and down.

6. Get climbing! Remember that you only count going up the stairs and when you have finished, you will actually have both ascended and descended the equivalent of the mountain that you have chosen.

BIBLE TO SHARE
MATTHEW 17:1-8 (Bible Overview 6)

Perhaps as you are halfway through your mountain climb, you might like to sit at the top of the stairs with a glass of water and read this story. To set the scene, explain that Peter has just declared that Jesus is the Messiah, and Jesus has spoken about his upcoming death.

Jesus climbed a mountain with Peter, James, and John, and there he was transfigured before them. This means that his appearance completely changed; his face shone like the sun, and his clothes were bright white like a blinding light. Moses and Elijah (two important people you may remember from other Bible stories) appeared there, talking with Jesus.

Not knowing what to say, Peter blurted out, 'Lord, it is good that we are here. Let's build three shelters – one for you, one for Moses, and one for Elijah.' Before he had finished this little speech, a bright cloud covered them, hushing him. A voice spoke from out of the cloud. 'This is my Son, whom I love. Listen to him!'

The disciples fell facedown, terrified. Jesus came over to them and touched them. 'Get up. Don't be afraid.' They looked up, and saw no-one but Jesus.

You might like to ask your child to imagine this scene!

QUESTIONS TO ASK ...

How do you feel walking up all these stairs?

I wonder what it felt like for the disciples on that mountaintop when they had just climbed the mountain?

Why do you think Peter wanted to build shelters or memorials on top of the mountain?

Jesus touches the disciples and tells them not to be afraid. What does this story show us about Jesus?

CONTINUED →

AGE RANGE: 5+
EFFORT LEVEL: 4/5
TIMING: 120+ MINS
VITAL EQUIPMENT: STAIRS, MOUNTAIN PICTURE, PEN AND PAPER, SPONSORSHIP FORM

A THOUGHT TO PONDER

Ever wondered why it's Moses and Elijah that Jesus meets with on the mountaintop? Moses represented the Law and Elijah represented the prophets. This gathering is another demonstration that Jesus came to fulfil the Law and the prophecies.

LET'S PRAY

As you continue climbing the stairs, why not put on a worship album and sing songs declaring how good Jesus is? Or you could try to think of a different thing to thank Jesus for every time you get to the top of the stairs! You could pretend you are on a mountaintop and shout these things whenever you get to the top.

Be careful on the stairs and I'd advise wearing (clean) trainers.

If you want to, you could also dress up!

ADVENTURE 52
Car Boot Sale

Every now and again, we have a bit of a sort-out at our house. One of my fondest childhood memories was decluttering our house, packaging up all the stuff and doing a car boot sale. With the opportunity to raise some extra pocket money, this can turn a tedious task into a mini adventure!

WHAT YOU DO:

1. Find a car boot sale in your area. Book a spot and get the date in the diary! If there is one you can visit beforehand, it can be a good idea to go along and scope out where is best to park your car. Near the food or by the entrance or exits is normally best.

2. Next, you need to have a good sort-out of stuff that you want to declutter from the home. You might like to turn this into a game. If you have a spare room to store the items, you can try meeting every ten minutes in the room. The first time, you each bring one item, the second time two items and so on, to see who can find the most things to get rid of.

3. Then you need to sort out the stock. There may be some things that need to be recycled rather than sold. Popular items that sell at a car boot sale include clothes, toys, ornaments, jewellery, baby goods, small furniture and books. If you have the time, give the items a quick clean and iron any clothing.

4. Once you have your items ready for sale, sort your products into categories (for example clothes, baby goods, toys) and price everything. You may want to do bargain buckets with all items inside costing £1 each.

5. Before the day, get some cash together for a float. A small bag or cash box is also useful for keeping the money safe.

6. Take some carrier bags and if you have a couple of fold-down tables, they will help you to display your goods. It's also worth packing a tarpaulin sheet just in case it rains for a brief period. Packing the car can be a challenge but do encourage your child to get stuck into as much of it as they can.

153

CONTINUED →

7. Arrive at the location early if you can, to secure a good spot and get your wares ready for sale.

8. Be friendly and remember that people often like to haggle at car boot sales, so be flexible with the prices.

9. Ask your child to help you count the money afterwards!

BIBLE TO SHARE
MATTHEW 21:12-13 (Bible Overview 6)

The Jewish Temple in Jerusalem was one of the marvels of the ancient world. It was a stunning piece of architecture but more importantly, it was the place that represented where God met with man. It was the holiest place a Jew could go and yet, rather than being a place of sacrifice and prayer, it had become a place of exploitation. It would cost two days' pay to enter and if there was a problem with your sacrifice, you would have to pay ten times the going rate for a different animal to sacrifice.

Jesus entered the temple during the feast of Passover and drove out all those who were buying and selling in the temple courts. He overturned the tables of the money-changers and the benches of those selling doves for sacrifice. He said to them, 'The Scriptures say, 'My house will be called a house of prayer', but you have made it a den of robbers!'

QUESTIONS TO ASK ...

What was it like sorting out your house and finding things to get rid of? Isn't it amazing how stuff builds up?

How do you think the Temple had got so bad?

What do you think holiness means?

Why do you think Jesus got so angry? How do you think the people reacted?

A THOUGHT TO PONDER

As Christians, we don't have a temple to go to but the Bible says that we are temples of the Holy Spirit (1 Corinthians 6:19). What might God want to drive out of our lives?

LET'S PRAY

Spend a moment in quiet, asking 'Jesus, what would you like me to get rid of in my life?' This might be an attitude in our heart, the way we behave, something we do – or something we own! Then ask him to help you get rid of it.

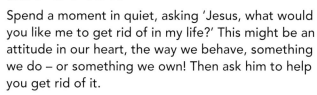

If there is no car boot sale nearby, you could try hosting a garage sale.

TOP TIPS

If you don't have a car, then is there someone else who could be up for joining you in this adventure?

AGE RANGE: 6+
EFFORT LEVEL: 5/5
TIMING: A FEW HOURS
VITAL EQUIPMENT: SOME THINGS TO SELL, CAR, FLOAT, TABLES OR TARPAULIN TO SHOWCASE YOUR PRODUCTS

FURTHER RESOURCES

AND

BIBLE OVERVIEW

Inspire a faith that lasts

THE KITCHEN TABLE PROJECT

If you've enjoyed these adventures, make sure you connect with us for more ideas and inspiration! Andy works closely with the Kitchen Table Project, which is a Care for the Family initiative that encourages and equips parents to inspire their children's faith.

1. Continue the journey

Sign up to receive regular encouragement and practical tips for having fun with your children and building their faith. Go to **kitchentable.org.uk/join**

2. Join our online community

Chat to other parents, share ideas and experiences, find out about everything that's going on and keep up to date with all our new resources.

    ktpcampaign

3. Check out more resources

Raising Faith by Katharine Hill and Andy Frost is packed with full-colour bite-sized articles and helpful ideas to try out in the busyness of life. This book will dispel the guilt and inspire you with new ways to help our children love God.

Inspire is an easy-to-run small group session that starts the conversation about nurturing faith in our kids. It's fun, relaxed and interactive. Why not gather a few friends together (in person, or online) to discuss it? Free to download. kitchentable.org.uk/inspire

Find these and more at **kitchentable.org.uk/resources**

CARE FOR THE FAMILY

Care for the Family is a national charity which aims to promote strong family life and help those who face family difficulties. Our work has been focused on the UK and the Isle of Man, but we are increasingly reaching a wider audience through digital technology.

We focus primarily on the following areas of family life: marriage/couple relationships, parenting and bereavement. Our aim is to be accessible to every family, whatever their circumstances, to provide support in difficult family situations, and to create resources that are preventative, evidence-based and easy to apply.

Visit our website to find out more about support for:
- Couple relationships
- Parenting
- Families with additional needs children
- Bereaved parents and siblings
- Single parents
- Young widows/widowers
- Parent and toddler groups
- Marriage preparation

cff.org.uk

For the latest news, event and training information, helpful articles and resources follow us online or get in touch.

029 2081 0800
mail@cff.org.uk

THE BIBLE

1. THE STORY BEGINS

Adam → Noah →

Abraham

Isaac ←

Jacob
(renamed Israel) →

Joseph

2. EGYPT TO THE PROMISED LAND

Moses

Joshua

3. ISRAEL

Judges
Ruth
Samuel
Saul
David
Solomon

4. ISRAEL DIVIDED

Israel   Judah

Elijah   Isaiah &
& Elisha   Jeremiah

5. CAPTIVITY & RETURN

Daniel
Esther

Nehemiah

6. JESUS

Matthew
Mark
Luke
John

12
Disciples

7. THE CHURCH

Peter/Paul
ACTS

WE'RE HERE!

8. REVELATION

HOPE

© Andy Frost and Daniel Watson
Share Jesus International